Identity

CHOICES

GUIDES FOR TODAY'S WOMAN

Identity

Ruth Tiffany Barnhouse

The Westminster Press
Philadelphia

Scripture quotations from the Revised Standard Version of the Bible are copyrighted 1946, 1952, © 1971, 1973 by the Division of Christian Education of the National Council of the Churches of Christ in the U.S.A. and are used by permission.

The quotations in Chapter 4 excerpted from the book *Mortal Stakes* by Robert B. Parker, copyright © 1975 by Robert B. Parker, are reprinted by permission of Delacorte Press/Seymour Lawrence.

Book design by Alice Derr

First edition

Published by The Westminster Press®
Philadelphia, Pennsylvania

PRINTED IN THE UNITED STATES OF AMERICA
9 8 7 6 5 4 3 2 1

Library of Congress Cataloging in Publication Data

Barnhouse, Ruth Tiffany, 1923–
   Identity.

   (Choices)
   Bibliography: p.
   1. Women—Psychology. 2. Identity (Psychology)
3. Feminism. 4. Family. 5. Woman (Christian theology)
I. Title. II. Series.
HQ1206.B27 1984   305.4′2   84-3664
ISBN 0-664-24545-5 (pbk.)

To my grandmother
Gertrude Kaufmann Tiffany
1871–1942

CONTENTS

PUBLISHER'S ACKNOWLEDGMENT

The publisher gratefully acknowledges the advice of several distinguished scholars in planning this series. Virginia Mollenkott, Arlene Swidler, Phyllis Trible, and Ann Ulanov helped shape the goals of the series, identify vital topics, and locate knowledgeable authors. Views expressed in the books, of course, are those of the individual writers and not of the advisers.

ACKNOWLEDGMENTS

I gratefully acknowledge my indebtedness to my family, my patients, and my friends, from whom I have learned nearly everything in this book; to Larry Daywitt for the wonderful phrase "naked and alone in a white room"; to Gerane West for holding the fort in Dallas while I escaped to Washington to write; to Sam Cook and Bill Hunnicutt for initiating me into the mysteries of the personal computer and word processor, without which this project would have taken at least another year; and to the College of Preachers in Washington, D.C., for providing me with a restful and inspiriting atmosphere in which to write.

R. T. B.

Washington, D.C.
November 1983

CHAPTER 1

What Do We Mean by "Identity"?

Identity is one of those peculiar words which, until asked to define it, we assume we understand. But once we begin to examine the concept, we realize it is far more complex than we first supposed. In this chapter we will look at some cultural factors that affect everyone's identity, men and women alike, in every time and place. We need to dig deeper than such dictionary definitions as "unity and persistence of personality" or "individuality; as, to forget one's *identity.*" The underlying question seems to be: "Who am I *really*?"

IDENTITY AND CULTURE

In former times people took their identity for granted. They were not troubled by the anxiety that accompanies so much of contemporary talk about the "search for identity." As recently as fifty years ago it was widely believed that God, or perhaps Fate, had assigned people to a particular "station in life" which they attempted to leave at their peril. Only trouble could come of trying to rise above, or sink below, one's destined station. Of course, at least in the United States, there was a romantic democratic fantasy that any baby *boy*, however humble in origin, could grow up to be President or win the Nobel Prize. This meant that we thought it was possible for *men* to change *their* station. It did not mean that we were abolishing the whole *idea* of station.

To our modern consciousness, the idea of a nearly immutable station in life seems unfair. We believe justice requires that everyone be able to advance as far as individual ability and opportunity permit. Recently we have begun to believe that society must provide opportunities for those formerly deprived of them, though we do not put this in practice very well as yet. We no longer believe that an "upward" change of station should be considered exceptional, or a "downward" change shameful. In fact, the whole idea of "upward" and "downward" is gradually disappearing as we espouse ever more egalitarian beliefs. This is reflected in such social customs as the common use of first names between employer and employee, professor and student, foreman and laborer, minister and parishioner, all of which would have been unthinkable only a generation ago. It is also reflected in new management styles that depend more and more on group collaboration rather than on the autocratic authority of one boss. Although in any such situation there is usually someone who is acknowledged to have the last word, modern notions of courtesy and fairness require all participants to have a hearing, whether their ideas are worth acting on or not.

Superficially this seems to be an unalloyed improvement over the old ways, not only for society at large but also for the individuals who compose it. In many respects that is true. But the changes have also introduced serious problems not anticipated by the reformers.

What happens when the idea of "station" is abolished? What happens when people are no longer brought up to "know their place" or to believe that trouble will come from "getting ideas above their station"? They lose an important part of their identity. They can no longer *identify* easily and securely with their background, since they are no longer expected to establish themselves in life by simply continuing their family and community traditions. It used to be common for young men to choose their father's occupation. In fact, "choose" is hardly the right word. It was simply assumed that they would. Nowadays such a decision is rarely automatic, and when it is, onlookers are likely to suspect inappropriately heavy parental influence. Each person is now urged to start from scratch, and many find themselves adrift in a sea of possibilities.

This degree of freedom can be intoxicating, and is welcome to some. But for many others, sooner or later it is confusing. The question "Who am I, really?" is now more difficult, since it can no longer be answered simply in terms of one's station or traditions. You will recall that the dictionary defined "identity" in terms of persistence. If *station* and *tradition* are no longer determining factors, if every circumstance is subject to change, what is it that persists? What is there to give the feeling of stable continuity so essential to a secure sense of identity?

IDENTITY AND OTHER PEOPLE

As social customs become increasingly egalitarian (at least superficially), the concept of friendship is eroding. A "friend" is now anyone you met yesterday with whom you are on speaking terms. Our grandparents would have called such people "acquaintances," reserving the term "friends" for those with whom they were truly intimate. They were not necessarily being snobbish. They were protecting themselves against the anxieties indicated in the modern saying that "you don't find out who your friends are until you're in trouble." Without clear distinctions between degrees of relationship, it is difficult to establish a sustaining network of intimacy.

We know that human beings are social by nature, but we are in danger of forgetting the significance of this truth. It does not mean that we only need others in various roles, principally to do those things we don't know how or have time to do for ourselves, like repair the washing machine or fix our teeth, or to do with us those things which cannot be done alone, like play tennis, run a business, or have sex. (There are, regrettably, some people who approach sex just that way.) Much more importantly, it means that we need enduring relationships with others which do not depend on their instrumental value. We not only need to receive affection but also to give it, including the need to touch and be touched at a basic level which has nothing to do with sex. Well-fed babies who are not held and fondled get sick. The rate of depression and physical illness among lonely, isolated widows and widowers is very high, but such persons often get better just through the simple expedient of acquiring a pet—a living creature who needs them, who will play with and touch them.

What did God say when he created Eve? "It is not good that the man should be alone." Contrary to what we have sometimes been told, Adam did not need Eve just to wash his socks and cook dinner. Presumably God could have trained a monkey to do that. Eve was needed for companionship, for intimacy, for true human sharing at every level. And she needed Adam for the same reason. Real intimacy with others implies taking the risk of being vulnerable, of letting them see you at your weakest and most ineffectual, even at your nastiest—not just when you are being good, strong, or successful. In such a network of true intimacy you are valued not only on your way up but when you are going nowhere or even down. Down and up, in any sense of those words, have nothing to do with it. But *time* does. There is no such thing as instant intimacy.

Success and achievement are valued much more highly in American culture than are friendship and intimacy. As we shall see in Chapter 4, this fact contributes both to the impoverishment of men and the devaluation of women. But children of both sexes are raised to believe that their future and their sense of identity depend on how well and how soon they learn to stand on their own two feet, which entails dissociating themselves from their natural network of intimacy. According to the Chinese-American anthropologist Francis L. K. Hsu, this means that children are motivated to seek independence from their parents long before they are ready for it. Parents tend to remain faithful, no matter how they are treated. But outsiders do not. Since there is constant premature, inept competition with peers for the status associated with independence, a pattern of mistrust is set up which, Dr. Hsu believes, "sets the tone of the Western man's approach to his fellow men for the rest of his life."

These problems are exaggerated in those parts of society where the divorce rate is 50 percent or more, since in those circumstances even parents cannot be relied on. There is good evidence to suggest that this high divorce rate is partly attributable to the fact that many spouses do not see one another primarily as sources of intimacy. That, as we have seen, always involves the possibility of putting up with unpleasantness. Instead they see one another as providers of happiness and convenience, to be discarded when they fail to come through, just as a business would change suppliers if the original company failed to deliver quality goods. In many schools, fewer than 25 percent of the children live with both natural parents. Growing up in such environments, even those from stable homes often have trouble developing a sense of permanence or continuity about *any* relationships. The influence of their own home may not be enough, since children form a large part of their concept of reality through interaction with their peers.

IDENTITY AND SELF

To find their center of identity, many people must now look within themselves to an extent never before required, though there were always some who chose to do so. Socrates thought that "the unexamined life is not worth living," and all methods of religious development have fostered as much self-knowledge as the student can tolerate. But Socrates was not speaking for everybody. Millions of people have lived fruitful lives without ever knowing themselves very deeply. The question about identity still principally means, even to many Americans, "How do I fit into the community of which I am a part?"

In our heart of hearts, each of us knows just how fragile we are, how totally unable to manage life without the caring support of others. In spite of that, contemporary values push us toward ever more self-sufficiency whether we are ready for it or not. Much of the root of the materialism and conspicuous consumption of our culture can be found in this tragic dilemma. As Dr. Hsu puts it, people begin to deal with their fundamental insecurity by "substituting material wealth for human intimacy," an enterprise that is doomed to fail. The notorious "mid-life crisis" and the devastating "retirement blues"—both of which are more frequent and more severe in our culture than in most others—are just two of the commoner manifestations of that failure.

THE PROBLEM OF BALANCE
BETWEEN INDIVIDUAL AND COMMUNITY

So far we have two radically different interpretations of the question. "Who am I, naked and alone in a white room?" Or, "Who am I in terms of my background and community?" Between these extremes lie many variations containing elements of both.

In complete isolation, identity is impossible. As proved by recent experiments, the literal answer to the question "Who am I, naked and alone in a white room?" is *nobody.* When *all* stimuli from the environment, physical as well as personal, are withdrawn, the subject becomes completely disoriented and begins to hallucinate in a matter of hours. The hallucinations are an attempt to supply the missing input, since the person cannot go on without it. No everyday life situation is that extreme. But difficulty in acquiring and maintaining a secure identity can be expected when even a few of the necessary supports are absent. Unfortunately, only after removing some of them in the name of progress have we begun to learn which ones (and how much) are necessary.

On the other hand, if identity is experienced *only* in terms of background and community, the individual is not really an individual but only an unreflecting member of a herd. We see this in crowd psychology and mass hysteria. Anyone who has ever experienced it knows how terrifying it can be to lose, under the powerful influence of the group, the sense of separate, critical ego and the ability to measure actions against one's own standards of morality or appropriateness. Even without such primitive extremes, people who do not experience themselves as distinct, deciding entities, well able to hold minority opinions, are easy prey for demagogues of all kinds. On a smaller scale, this danger is regularly displayed in the behavior of children and adolescents, whose sense of personal identity is still in formation. It is sometimes very hard for them to resist peer pressure, even when they know that what the group proposes is unacceptable. The ringleader is usually stronger, more intelligent, or more mature than the rest and from this position can manipulate the group with ease.

The solution to the American dilemma does not, therefore, lie in trying to recapture the stage where the social unit is paramount, and individuals must submerge their own needs and desires in its service. That too is destructive of personal identity. There are some cultures organized along those lines. In the United States, and to a considerable degree in most other Western countries, the emphasis is on individualism. But in the countries which we perceive as totalitarian, such as the Soviet Union, the emphasis is on the collective. We are horrified by their suppression of individual rights. But they are horrified by what they perceive in us as untrammeled personal selfishness bordering on social anarchy, favoring the strong at the expense of the weak.

In practice things are not so simple. There are numerous factors that characterize a culture. Many of these are extremely subtle, perhaps defying any analysis. But in all cultures the relationship of personal identity to group identity is evident, and always centrally important. It is in continuous interaction with all the other factors, modifying and being modified by them. These include such things as systems of trade, beliefs about sexual roles, educational practices, availability and use of natural resources—the list is almost endless.

In spite of the fact that it is often ignored, a good case can be made for the idea that this tension between the needs and rights of the individual and the needs and rights of the community is *the* central human problem. In a well-functioning society these two poles are in balance, neither drastically outweighing the other in importance or influence. Some intuition of this is contained in the common saying, "One for all and all for one." The crucial point is that serious lack of balance, *in either direction,* is detrimental to the full flourishing of personal identity.

Another way of putting it is to say that people cannot realize their potential if they have either too little or too much freedom. But that formulation is often hard for Americans to grasp because freedom is perhaps our highest national ideal. Devotion to that ideal makes us forget that you can have too much of a good thing. There is an ancient Chinese book of wisdom, the *I Ching,* which puts the case very well:

> In human life ... the individual achieves significance through discrimination and the setting of limits. Therefore what concerns us here is the problem of clearly defining these discriminations, which are, so to speak, the backbone of morality. *Unlimited possibilities are not suited to man; if they existed, his life would only dissolve in the boundless. To become strong, a man's life needs the limitations ordained by duty and voluntarily accepted.* The individual attains significance as a free spirit only by surrounding himself with these limitations and by determining for himself what his duty is. (P. 232, emphasis added)

Our danger is clearly that of unlimited possibilities. "The sky is the limit" is a peculiarly American idea. In some other countries the danger is that of limitations which are ordained not by self-determined duty but by government, and which are enforced rather than voluntarily accepted.

How do such serious imbalances arise? One important cause is the old mistake of substituting means for ends. Neither freedom nor order is an appropriate end in itself.

But both are essential means of establishing a functional society in which individuals can flourish.

Probably no society has ever handled this problem exactly right. But some have clearly done better than others. At present there appears to be an unusual amount of imbalance in most parts of the world. This is hard on everybody and contributes significantly to the current threat of an unimaginably disastrous war. All parties to the conflict are vigorously attacking the obvious imbalance in the others, and none are doing very much about correcting their own. The optimistic interpretation is that humanity is having growing pains and that before things get entirely unmanageable some balance will be restored.

HOW MATURE IS THE HUMAN RACE?

Growing pains? We left the Garden of Eden long ago, but have not yet arrived in the Kingdom of Heaven. How far have we come? Is there any way to find out? There are good biological reasons to believe that the development of individuals, from the moment of fertilization to maturity, recapitulates fairly accurately in miniature the evolution of our species since its beginnings billions of years ago. Since the body and the psyche are indissolubly bound together, this principle must apply not only to biological development but also to the development of consciousness. It follows that if we consider the psychological process through which a human child grows from infancy to maturity, we may learn something about the general growth of the whole human race.

At first infants do not experience themselves as separate from their mothers any more than you and I experience ourselves as separate from, say, our liver or our lungs. This corresponds with primitive cultures, which anthropologists believe to have been matriarchal. This means that the members of the group did not experience themselves as individuals with a unique personal destiny but as members of a collective. If we consider the creation accounts in Genesis as describing in symbolic and poetic form the origin of our species, we may compare this infancy stage with the description of Adam and Eve in the Garden of Eden, before the Fall. They were at home with nature and God, so unself-conscious that even clothes were not necessary.

At about two years of age, give or take a few months, the child begins to develop a will of its own and for the first time says "No!" to Mother. This is an essential stage in the development of personal identity, but it also causes a good deal of trouble. We may compare this to the Fall. God had endowed Adam and Eve with what theologians call "free will," and they abused it. (I like to think that without the malicious temptation by the serpent, God would in his own time, when Adam and Eve were ready, have found a way to teach us how to use his gift of free will without abusing it in the sinful ways which have characterized human development ever since. But we are stuck with what is, not enjoying what might have been.)

Older children *gradually* learn rules. But for a long time they follow those rules not because they understand them, and have consciously decided to accept the principles on which they rest, but because authority (usually parental) tells them to. This corresponds to the long period of human history during which the king or emperor reigned supreme, having full power of life and death over his subjects. Often God was thought to speak directly only to the ruler and high priests, instructions being passed down the chain of command through heads of households, with women, children, and slaves simply doing what they were told without question. It is this patriarchal period from which we have recently begun to emerge.

By adolescence, children have reached a confusing and contradictory stage. On the one hand, they want freedom to make decisions for themselves, to be thought of as responsible, independent persons. That is why they often reject parental authority or advice, even when they know the advice is good and secretly might like to take it. On the other hand, they are frightened of this much freedom and tend to huddle together in packs. They respond strongly to peer pressure and are often intensely miserable if they feel unaccepted by their group. They do not yet really know how to stand alone when that is desirable. This ambivalence is hard to bear and often is expressed in inconsistent behavior. For example, in some schools pupils are still required to wear uniforms. When that is the case, each child tries, right up to the limit of the dress code, to find some way to look different from the others. But in schools where there is no dress code, fashions come and go, and woe betide the young person who is wearing red socks when everybody else's are white!

The emphasis on freedom and personal rights for *everyone*, not just kings and the upper classes, is very new in human history. Our own American Revolution was one of the first major manifestations of that trend in the Western world. As indicated earlier in this chapter, different countries are proceeding toward that idea in different ways and at different rates, and each group tends to insist that its own way is the best. A comparison with the kind of competition that one sees between rival groups of adolescents is hard to resist.

Individual human beings do, of course, progress beyond this point. Recognizing that the goal can never be fully or consistently realized, I shall describe the mature state as that in which one is so confident of one's own identity and worth that one can give freely without feeling diminished and receive without a sense of anxious obligation. Furthermore, one has developed one's perceptions of internal as well as external reality and the intellectual and moral assessments of those realities to the point where one can make honest mistakes without a crippling sense of guilt and can enjoy personal successes without the distortion of pride. A profound sense of responsibility can be expected to flow naturally from those who have made significant progress along the road to such a goal.

Many individuals do make such progress. But it is perfectly obvious that the human race *as a whole*, particularly when acting in large groups, is at best adolescent. There seems to be something about belonging to a large group that makes us regress far below the level of behavior which we expect of ourselves and others in private life. Our standards and values may be very high when we are acting as Mary Smith or John Jones. But when we are acting not as individuals but in one of our *roles*—business executive, factory worker, government official, taxpayer, religious reformer, or whatever—our standards are almost always lower. People attempting to function publicly to the same high standard they bring to private behavior are usually told they are "not being realistic" or that they are "too idealistic for the real world." The larger the group, and the farther away from daily experience those on the other side of the question are, the worse our behavior becomes.

We often hear that "it's a dog-eat-dog world out there," and "out there" refers to the public, rather than the private, arena. Arena is just the right word: it's where the lions ate the Christians. It would be as accurate to say, "It's a toddlers-fighting-over-the-toys-in-the-sandbox world out there," and perhaps thinking of it that way might make us pay more attention to how we are actually behaving.

Whatever we choose to call it, it is certainly *not* the

Kingdom of Heaven. That Kingdom necessarily must include *everybody* and cannot be characterized by islands of pretty good private behavior surrounded by alligator-filled swamps of public suspicion and hostility. Instead, it will surely be composed of fully conscious, mature individuals who form together a truly cooperative community. We are not there yet. We are caught in racial adolescence, somewhere between the Garden of Eden and the Kingdom of Heaven. Even as individuals our identity is not firmly grounded, since under group pressure, prejudice, fear, insecurity, or a host of other factors we fall away from the best that we know. Very few people escape this trap, and those who do are recognized as saints.

We conclude this chapter with a lively paradox. There is no individuality apart from community, since isolation from intimate, enduring relationships with others leads to disorders of personhood. But it is also true that you cannot participate creatively and responsibly in community without knowing who you are as a separate, individual child of God. To arrive at a satisfactory answer to the question "Who am I, *really?*" you have to learn to balance these extremes.

REFERENCES

Hsu, Francis L. K., "Kinship Is the Key," *The Center Magazine*, November/December 1973, pp. 4–14. This eye-opening view of our culture is more than worth a trip to the library.

Wilhelm, Richard, *The I Ching*, trans. by Cary F. Baynes. 3d ed. Princeton University Press, 1968.

CHAPTER 2

What's Special
About Women's Identity?

In the last chapter we examined some of the factors that affect the formation of any person's identity, regardless of sex. In this chapter we will consider how the ancient idea of male supremacy causes a woman's identity to differ significantly from that of a man.

WOMAN'S SECONDARY STATION

Because we live in a world that has been largely patriarchal for about eight thousand years, women have not been thought about very much except in terms of how they affect men's lives. It is fashionable to suppose that they have always and everywhere been painfully oppressed, but that is not true. Nevertheless, the needs, wishes, characteristics, and attitudes of men have always been paramount. Women have been appreciated principally for those traits which give reproductive and social support to men's ambition.

There have been exceptions. Queen Elizabeth I, who ruled England from 1558 to 1603, is among the most illustrious, and she presided over one of that country's finest periods of development. She is often referred to as the Virgin Queen. That title may or may not be accurate as to physical virginity, but it certainly does describe the way she functioned. She decided not to marry, though she had many ardent suitors. She thought marriage would compromise her authority, without which she could not rule her country successfully. It is hard to imagine that she feared her own capitulation to a husband's opinions, but she certainly thought that her subjects would be in doubt about who was actually making the decisions. She could not take that risk, especially since England had been through a great deal of turmoil in the years just before her coronation. We can see how much progress has been made in the hundred and fifty years of the gradual rise of feminism when we consider that nobody imagines that the husbands of Mrs. Margaret Thatcher, England's current Prime Minister, or Mrs. Sandra Day O'Connor, a justice of our own Supreme Court, are influencing the way they do their jobs.

Such outstanding, individualistic development of women's personhood remains rare. The interesting question is why? The answer lies importantly in the institution of patriarchy. As we shall see in the next chapter, there are also reasons connected with the apparently innate differences between men and women. But these would not have prevented women from flourishing on their own terms except in a hierarchical society that took male supremacy for granted.

A woman's station was derived from that of her father and could only be changed (either up or down) through marriage. Her new station was always that of her husband. A man could marry below his station without endangering the status of his children, though it was generally considered bad taste. But a woman who married below her station of origin was affecting not only herself but her children, since their station would derive from that of their father.

Women were seldom free to pick their own husbands.

Marriages were often arranged by families and in any case had to be approved. Usually women could refuse a suggested mate, but to do so was perilous, since to be single was often an economic burden and in some places a disgrace. Considerate parents protected their daughters by preventing them from meeting men who would not be acceptable husbands. Once married, a woman was expected to conform to her husband's circumstances—for better or for worse—and to refrain from any behavior that would embarrass him or interfere with his comfort.

Men's freedom was also restricted, since the accident of birth was largely determinative in a way most of us can now hardly imagine. (*To those in some minority groups this problem is still all too real.*) But within that constraint, men could choose among the available options. Women, on the other hand, were far more restricted. Their range of choice, while in individual instances great, was always contingent on patriarchal approval. Women who were observant enough of society and of themselves to understand this, and to recognize their own independent career ambitions, had to forgo the pleasures of marriage and motherhood. In most instances they also had to endure some degree of social disapproval to reach their goals. Not many were courageous enough for all that, which accounts for the relative scarcity of famous women up to the present.

Even more important is the fact that the very idea of figuring out an independent answer to the question "Who am I, really?", an answer that did not depend on being someone's daughter, wife, or mother, simply did not occur to most women. But, as we shall see, this did not mean that they were mere cyphers, passively going along with the dictates of their menfolk, never having any ideas or values of their own.

AGATHA CHRISTIE AND OTHER VICTORIANS

How did these customs, so strange to us now, work out in real life? No single answer is possible. But let us take one particularly articulate example, Agatha Christie. She was born in 1891 and lived until 1976. She began writing her autobiography in 1950 and worked on it intermittently until 1965. By the time she was born, the early feminists had already done a great deal both in England and the United States, so the old standards had begun to loosen. Queen Victoria reigned, which had a subtly favorable effect on the position of women in England as compared with other European countries. But during Christie's lifetime there were many more changes, and she died in a completely different world from the one into which she was born. In a fascinating passage, she describes her feelings at about age twelve.

> In fact I only contemplated one thing—a happy marriage. About that I had complete self-assurance—as all my friends did. We were conscious of all the happiness that awaited us; we looked forward to love, to being looked after, to being cherished, and admired, and we intended to get our own way in the things which mattered to us while at the same time putting our husbands' life, career and success before all, as was our proud duty. (Agatha Christie, *An Autobiography*, p. 145)

To appreciate that passage, we must recall that duty was far more highly regarded then than it is now. It would be hard to find a contemporary author who would use the word "proud" to describe it. She goes on:

> The real excitement of being a girl—of being, that is, a woman in embryo—was that life was such a wonderful gamble. *You didn't know what was go-*

ing to happen to you. That was what made being a woman so exciting. No worry about what you should be or do—Biology would decide. You were waiting for The Man, and when the man came, he would change your entire life! You can say what you like, that is an exciting point of view to hold at the threshold of life. What will happen? "Perhaps I shall marry someone in the Diplomatic Service . . . I think I should like that; to go abroad and see all sorts of places. . . ." Or: "I don't think I would like to marry a sailor; you would have to spend such a lot of time living in seaside lodgings." Or: "Perhaps I'll marry someone who builds bridges, or an explorer." The whole world was open to you—not open to your *choice;* but open to what Fate *brought* you. You might marry *anyone;* you might, of course, marry a drunkard or be very unhappy, but that only heightened the general feeling of excitement. And one wasn't marrying the profession, either; it was the *man.* (P. 146)

Her man, Archie Christie, is portrayed as a singularly selfish person who eventually left her for another woman. Not approving of divorce, she was willing to continue the marriage in spite of that betrayal. She takes much of the blame for what went wrong, feeling that if she had stayed with him instead of going to her mother's house for several months his attention might not have strayed. She says this in spite of the fact that her reason for going was that her adored mother had died, and someone was needed to sort the possessions and settle the estate. She had begged him to accompany her, but he refused, partly because he found being around grief depressing! She never realistically confronted him with the unacceptability of his behavior. Why not? It never occurred to her to question the underlying idea that the man was to be "head of the house," and she believed that happiness was not possible on any other basis. His wishes, there-

fore, always took precedence over hers. She could suggest, she could request, but she could *insist* only in an
emergency, and then more easily for her child than for
herself. In the current phrase, our consciousness has
been raised, and relatively few women nowadays would
accept Archie Christie's behavior.

Writing in her old age, she considers the changes she
has witnessed and comments as follows:

> The position of women, over the years, has defi-
> nitely changed for the worse. We women have be-
> haved like mugs. . . .
>
> It seems sad that having established ourselves
> so cleverly as the "weaker sex," we should now be
> broadly on a par with the women of primitive tribes
> who toil in the fields all day, walk miles to gather
> camel-thorn for fuel, and on trek carry all the pots,
> pans and household equipment on their heads,
> while the gorgeous, ornamental male sweeps on
> ahead, unburdened save for one lethal weapon with
> which to defend his women.
>
> You've got to hand it to Victorian women, they got
> their menfolk where they wanted them. They es-
> tablished their frailty, delicacy, sensibility—their
> constant need of being protected and cherished.
> Did they lead miserable, servile lives, downtrodden
> and oppressed? Such is not *my* recollection of them.
> All my grandmother's friends seem to me in retro-
> spect singularly resilient and almost invariably suc-
> cessful in getting their own way. They were tough,
> self-willed, and remarkably well read and well in-
> formed.
>
> . . . They genuinely thought men were splendid
> fellows—dashing, inclined to be wicked, easily led
> astray. [*That sentence helps to explain why Christie
> was so willing to take the blame for her husband's
> outrageous behavior.*] In daily life a woman got her
> own way while paying due lip service to male su-

periority, so that her husband should not lose face.
(Pp. 149–150)

Christie's career was fabulously successful. She wrote
more than eighty novels and a number of plays. It is
surprising, therefore, to learn that she never really
thought of herself as an author. Even when she was well
over forty, in a happy second marriage, it didn't occur to
her to describe herself as anything but a "married
woman" (the English term for "housewife"). She thought
of that as her primary occupation, her writing being
something she did on the side. Not until the money
began to roll in was she confronted with her professional
identity, and even then it remained secondary.

To the end of her life she put her family first, assisting
her second husband, Sir Max Mallowan, on his archaeo-
logical expeditions to the Middle East by carefully clean-
ing and photographing the finds. But even here she
underestimated herself. She once told him sadly that she
wished she had studied archaeology, and his astonished
reply was to remind her that she knew more about pre-
historic pottery than practically any other woman in England.

Christie's story illustrates very well the special nature
of women's identity and the dilemma of modern women
as they attempt to grapple with it. Fortunately for the
millions who enjoy her entertaining books, neither of her
husbands disapproved of her writing. Archie was so self-
centered that he was glad of any activity that could keep
her amused while he pursued his own ends, and besides,
he liked the extra money. Max appreciated her for what
she was and encouraged her for that reason. But, by her
own account, if either of them had not liked her to write,
she would probably have given it up.

Christie was not alone in approving of her era. In 1861,
Catherine Beecher and her sister Harriet Beecher Stowe

published a book, called *The American Woman's Home*, which covered every conceivable aspect of that topic. In over five hundred closely packed pages they discuss everything; homesite selection and architecture, hygiene and simple medicine, child-rearing (including education), kitchen gardens and cooking, management of household help, duties to the poor, the importance of spending time every day on personal intellectual and spiritual development—all these and more are covered. There is *not one word* in the whole book on how to get your husband to like any of it. In fact, husbands are not even mentioned. This underscores the point that women had enormous power in their own sphere and had far more scope for the expression and development of individual talent and preference in the home than they do now.

In those days women not only took pride in but were appreciated for the development and maintenance of human relationships, both in the family and in the community. It is no accident that the first all-male profession they entered in significant numbers was teaching, followed closely by medicine. They had an easier time with the former, since the education of children in school was easily perceived as a natural extension of education in the home. But medicine was not far behind. Few realize that in 1900 5.6 percent of all the doctors in the United States were women. The highest percentage was in Boston, which had 18 percent, followed by Chicago with 13 percent. (Walsh, *Journal of the American Medical Women's Association.*) One *male* feminist, Prof. O. S. Fowler, wrote in 1870 that "in teaching and doctoring women are naturally men's superiors." He was generalizing from his view of women as sympathetic, intuitively inclined to protect and nourish life.

But women's progress was more extensive still. At the 1876 centennial celebration in Philadelphia, there was a popular Woman's Pavilion celebrating their achievements. And a book was published giving short biographies of about five hundred notable women, active in all walks of life. Anticipating developments in England by over fifty years, liberal arts colleges for women were founded. The first, in 1861, was begun by a man, Matthew Vassar. All these advances proceeded with the approval of benevolent patriarchs, patriarchy itself not yet having been questioned. It continued to be assumed that the natural thing was for women to marry, and to take an attitude toward their husbands similar to that of Agatha Christie.

Many women in the same era were dissatisfied. Those are the ones most frequently quoted in modern feminist literature. But a culture cannot be properly understood unless we hear not only from those who found it burdensome but also from those who appreciated it. It matters that there were *women*—competent, successful women— not just men, who liked the old ways. And yet, we can see from Christie's example the effect of those ways on her sense of identity.

MODERN DEVELOPMENTS

Nearly everything has changed since then. Feminism is coming in like the tide, each wave bringing new progress (as well as problems!) in spite of temporary losses between waves. Modern researchers, trying to study women *as they are in themselves,* in a way they have never been studied before, find—often to their surprise—that, in any society, women define themselves in terms of their relationships with other people far more than men do. Even young, modern, thoroughly feminist women show this tendency. There is good evidence that this is to some degree innate, even though under patriarchy the way women were raised served to reinforce it while simultaneously suppressing other, more self-determining attitudes. In terms of the issue raised in the last chapter, women tend to focus on the values of community (though almost always on a small scale), while men tend to focus on the values of individualism.

This view has received important recent support from research done at Harvard by the psychologist Carol Gilligan. The subjects of her experiment were presented with moral dilemmas and asked to choose an outcome, giving reasons for their choice. For example, should a man steal a drug he cannot afford in order to save his wife's life? The druggist has already been asked to lower the price but has refused. As early as age twelve, males and females see this problem differently. Boys see a conflict between life and property and try to solve the problem with logic. Girls see a disturbance in human relationships, which must be approached in personal terms. The rest of Gilligan's research shows that women are more concerned with *responsibility toward relationships,* and men with the *rights of individuals.*

The questions were taken from scales designed to measure degrees of moral and social development. The originator, Lawrence Kohlberg (also from Harvard), found that women generally scored lower than men, and, when tested after a lapse of time, often seemed to have dropped back. But Gilligan knew that these scales were developed using only male subjects. Since in other respects the women did not seem immature, she decided to investigate further, suspecting that the criteria that apply to men might not be relevant to women's maturation. Prior to Gilligan's work, the interpretation of women's responses was that they were morally less developed than men because they did not assess dilemmas primarily in terms of theoretical conflicts of rights, as men tend to do. This judgment is not surprising, since the test was devised by men and all the research subjects were male.

Naturally they would look at it in their own terms. Criticizing this defect, Gilligan says:

> To the question, "What does he see that she does not?" Kohlberg's theory provides a ready response . . . ; to the question, "What does she see that he does not?" Kohlberg's theory has nothing to say.
> (Carol Gilligan, *In a Different Voice*, p. 31)

Such glaring failures to pay real attention to women have been interpreted by some feminists to support their contention that patriarchy has always and everywhere been oppressive and that men do not care about women so long as their own needs are met. This is demonstrably untrue. Many influential men have been active in the feminist movement from its beginnings in the last century, and when women finally got the vote, it was men who voted to give it to them. Of course there have always been selfish people of either sex who were interested in nothing except getting their own way as often as possible. And it is probably true that, given the generally accepted idea of male supremacy, it has been easier for men than for women to get away with such behavior.

PROBLEMS IN LETTING GO OF PATRIARCHY

Because we have learned to question male supremacy, we feel oppressed in situations that our grandmothers would have experienced quite differently. In evaluating the past, we must be careful not to attribute reactions to people in former generations which do not fit with the cultural beliefs prevailing at the time, accepted by women as well as by men. In fact, "accepted" is hardly even the right word. These ideas were completely taken for granted. You are not "accepting" something that it has never even crossed your mind not to accept. It just *is*.

If we are to grapple successfully with the complex

problems of contemporary culture, importantly characterized by being somewhere in the middle of a transition
out of eight thousand years of patriarchy to some future,
totally new way, it is absolutely essential to understand
that point. If we do *not* understand it, we are likely to
"throw the baby out with the bathwater." Everybody
who lived before the second half of the twentieth century
was not necessarily either a tyrant or a victim. And I have
a far better opinion of women than to suppose that they
were either stupid or silly enough to put up with anything for eight thousand years unless there was something in it for them. What might that have been? One
answer is obvious. Though contemporary feminists now
see such customs as sexist, many women really did enjoy
being protected by men against the vicissitudes of life
that men had to endure. It may well have been a fair
exchange for the risks women took in childbearing, risks
now all but obliterated by modern medicine.

But I think there is another answer, one far more
important. Women were willing to give up a good deal of
freedom to get out of the corresponding amount of responsibility. Under patriarchy, women were *never* in the
position expressed by the saying, "The buck stops here!"
When men made mistakes, women could think that if
only they had been running things, they would have
done a better job—but such musings were never put to
the test. Messes were never women's fault. When things
went well, they could take credit for having married a
competent man or for having given him excellent suggestions. They could think of themselves as "the power
behind the throne," but it's worth remembering that
when something goes wrong it's the king who loses his
head. If you live in a society that requires male permission for every course of action, you may accomplish a
great deal if you are clever enough, and if you are lucky
enough in the men from whom that permission must be

obtained. But women never had full responsibility for any decision, not even the ones made in their primary sphere, the home, because men always had veto power. Even the undoubted power we saw that women had in the home was delegated to them by men. Considering that fact, together with women's natural tendency to pay attention *first* to the integrity of the network of relationships, you have some extremely powerful forces at work *from the women's side, not just from the men's,* to keep the patriarchal system going.

Even now there are women who want to get back to the "good old days." Others want to scrap the past entirely and start over from square one, some going so far as to declare that men are the enemy. Neither group understands how cultural changes actually come about. Changes that work for the benefit of all come through the patient development of an educated consensus, combined with an optimistic willingness to risk trying something new for the sake of a better future, never forgetting that the new edifice must be built on the foundations of the past.

In the last chapter I pointed out that in our culture success and achievement are more highly valued than friendship and intimacy. We can now see how for women that statement needs to be qualified. In a patriarchal culture the professed, public values are those of men. Lots of women feel free to encourage or even to push their husbands toward success. For themselves it is a different story. A disproportionate number of women find the necessary competition anxiety provoking, and many fail just when the goal is in sight. This happens most often to women who are trying to enter predominantly male professions where the men against whom they must compete are all engaged in the fiercest cutthroat competition. Do you notice the violence in that common phrase? That is exactly what gets to many women who try to imitate it. Something in them rebels at the last minute, even when they are ardent feminists and have a genuine interest in the work. Naturally their male classmates or colleagues, even when well-meaning and friendly, cannot understand what is wrong or help them in any way. Usually the women themselves don't know what it is. This is because without thinking about it they have bought into the culture's nearly unqualified admiration of success and achievement at any cost. Not until they have hands-on experience with what that actually entails does the conflict with their feminine sensibilities erupt.

Why is it so difficult for these women to become aware of their own feelings? They have believed the prevailing view that their natural urge to compassion is mere sentimentality, which may be all right in intimate social life or in the circumscribed field of "good works" but has no place in the hardheaded world of business. Displays of emotion are considered out of place in that arena, with the single exception of angry outbursts by males, designed to intimidate and control their professional inferiors. Anger from women ·in similar circumstances is rarely accepted. It is perceived as hysterical, as evidence that women in such positions are really not reliable. The old view of women as sweet smoothers of the man's path is still with us. Women trying to function in that man's world, then, are prevented from acting out of their own feminine core but are also impeded when they try to imitate the male style. Thus, as Gilligan puts it, "women come to question the normality of their feelings and to alter their judgments in deference to the opinion of others." The masculine way of doing things is seen as strong, and therefore admirable, while their own tendency to prize caring and empathy is devalued as weak.

I have used the world of work outside the home to illustrate the problems, but that is not the only place they surface. Many kinds of familial discord can be traced to the relational quality of women's identity, we will consider those in later chapters. All women do not succumb to these problems. Some happy combination of intuition, shrewdness, and temperament enables many to proceed with outstanding success, maintaining their own balance through all the hazards. But we can safely claim that there are two special aspects to women's identity. The first is their fundamental concern with the network of relationships. The second is the tendency to subscribe to public masculine values to an extent that makes it hard for them to evaluate their own needs and strengths. Even the strongest of us still has one foot in the patriarchal system, whether we know it or not.

References

Christie, Agatha, *Agatha Christie, an Autobiography.* Ballantine Books, 1978. I can think of no better way to get a vivid sense of the change we are all caught up in than to read this book. It is not only thought-provoking but also extremely entertaining.

Fowler, Prof. O. S., *Creative and Sexual Science, Including Manhood, Womanhood and their Mutual Interrelations, LOVE, its Laws, Power Etc.* National Publishing Co., 1870. This quaint, out-of-print book expounds a view we do not ordinarily associate with Victorians. If you can find a copy, you will find its combination of prophetic insistence on woman's equality and outmoded mistakes about the psychology of both men and women both fascinating and entertaining.

Gilligan, Carol, *In a Different Voice.* Harvard University Press, 1982. This is one of the most important books of the last ten years—maybe more than that. It is accessible to the general reader and has an excellent bibliography, useful to those wishing to delve deeper into this crucial subject.

CHAPTER 3

Why Is Finding Personal Identity Hard for Women?

One answer to why women have difficulty in finding personal identity is their subsidiary role under patriarchy. But there are others, related not only to the way women have been socialized but also to what appear to be innate differences between men and women. Before discussing what those may be, however, we need to consider in more detail how some of the issues already mentioned affect individuals.

IDENTITY PROBLEMS OF INDIVIDUALS

At the close of Chapter 1 we saw that *separate individuality* and *membership in community* must be balanced in order to discover and maintain true identity. Without a firm grounding in a safe social network, it is nearly impossible to find out who one might be *individually,* since that requires some exploration of the unknown and enough self-confidence to take the risk of being different. Children's need for this kind of security is well known, but adults need it too. After World War II, business in this country developed policies that uprooted executives and their families every two years or so and set them down in a new place, not of their own choosing, with no friends or familiar circumstances. They had the right to refuse, but this was more apparent than real, since men (and it was always *men*) who did not accept these assignments generally lost their chance of future advancement. But recent research into the degree of stress induced by various common events has shown that moving is second only to the death of a spouse. Our whole society is now paying the price for this mistake, which has contributed to a generation of alienated children of the affluent and a veritable epidemic of stress diseases and alcoholism among their parents.

People whose identity is almost exclusively based in their social connections also suffer. There is no sense of personal responsibility, no initiative is taken, and emotional collapse in a crisis is likely. Such people go beyond being just followers, they become parasites. Others, whose temperament is livelier, may suffer from thwarted ambition. This may be expressed in petty tyranny, depression, psychosomatic illness, or other manifestations of psychological pain. Those tied to a group that does not even give them a pleasant sense of security may develop more extreme disorders. Modern feminists contend that the development of women's personal identity has been thwarted in precisely these ways, and there is a great deal of truth in what they say.

In Chapter 2 we discovered that under patriarchy women are seriously discouraged, when not actually prevented, from exploring the full extent of their separateness. Their sphere of activity and influence has been largely restricted to the family and intimate social circle. This is true even when, under economic necessity, they have had to work outside the home. The differences between men and women were systematically emphasized in such a way as to cause everyone to believe that women were truly inferior to men—if not totally, then at least in those qualities required to manage public life.

It takes no great power of observation to notice that men have not done a particularly good job in managing public life, either. In fact, that was one of the strong arguments for giving women the vote—it was hoped that their superior moral influence would improve the conduct of government. Unfortunately that hope was based on far too simplistic an interpretation of the differences between men and women and overlooked almost entirely the influence of patriarchal conditioning for thousands of years. It assumed that women were morally superior, that they would have no trouble knowing and asserting who they were *in themselves*, and that men would welcome their doing so! But women do have trouble, and the question is why? Attempting an answer requires a careful look at the actual differences between men and women and at the effect of these differences in the conduct of daily life.

MEN AND WOMEN ARE NOT ALIKE

Some feminists believe that there are no innate differences between men and women other than the purely biological. Their argument is that apparent differences all result from patriarchally inspired efforts to socialize women into subordination. The historical as well as the contemporary evidence showing the pervasiveness of sexual stereotyping as a powerful factor in determining how children of each sex will be socialized and educated is truly impressive. The process begins in the cradle, pink for girls and blue for boys, and goes on inexorably from there: dolls for girls, toy guns and cars for boys. This differential treatment continues right into adult life, and it is not surprising that some thoughtful people examining these data conclude that *all* psychological differences between men and women can be traced to such influences.

Such beliefs were prevalent about twelve years ago, when the wording of the Equal Rights Amendment was designed. As Phyllis Schlafly documents in her book *The Power of the Positive Woman*, many efforts were made to include a qualifying phrase, one that would acknowledge sexual differences and permit account to be taken of them in some circumstances. But proponents of the amendment believed that any admission of innate difference either was or might be construed as evidence of inferiority. Of course nobody imagined that the inferiority might be attributed to men!

The present psychological position of women is perhaps at an all-time low. To be sure, advances have been made on the legal front: women can own property, can demand (in most places) equal pay for equal work, establish their own credit, and so forth. But in other respects, things are much worse. Traditionally women excelled at motherhood and homemaking and were highly appreciated by all for these accomplishments. Now, however, those activities are widely devalued, and many women, when asked what they do, reply, "I'm *only* a housewife." How different from Agatha Christie's proud claim to be a "married woman"! Perhaps this contemporary devaluation of women is why so many are tempted to believe that men and women are alike. Women have unconsciously accepted the false idea of male supremacy and see no way out of their present social and spiritual dilemmas other than to assert that women are in fact the same as men.

But we are confronted with some stubborn facts. Nobody who has even a passing familiarity with the animal kingdom would deny that there are clear behavioral differences between male and female that are not directly connected with the reproductive process. It is hardly likely that human beings are the only exception to this rule. Further, every known culture, past or present, has assumed a fundamental difference, and I do not believe that could be a universal phenomenon if it did not have some basis in fact. At the same time, there is an astonishing variety in the specific roles assigned to each sex in different societies. Each culture, sometimes each *sub-culture*, tends to view its own customs as a concrete manifestation of an obvious eternal truth about the sexes. Our own is no exception.

When we try to think seriously about the real differences, it becomes extremely important to remember that the sexual is only *one* component of anyone's identity. No complete list of the other factors is possible, but some obvious ones follow: chronological age, maturity, physical health, occupation, religion, education, social class, family relationships, emotional and mental stability, intelligence, nationality, and culture. Also very important is psychological type (such things as whether the person is introverted or extroverted, primarily a logical or a feeling type, intuitive or practical). All these factors are in continuous interaction with one another, and the extent of their influence varies not only from one situation to another but from time to time in the same person. Some are permanent, some change. Some tend to have a subtle effect on all of the others most of the time, while others are only occasionally important.

The most damaging influence of stereotypes of any kind is that they single out one *of these many factors and make it decisive for how a person should behave or be treated by others.* This does violence to the true complexity of everyone's identity. To the extent that stereotypes have influenced people's view of themselves, their own sense of identity is distorted. Once the stereotype has been identified as harmful, as is now the case for sexual stereotypes, it becomes very difficult to determine what the *real* influence of the factor in question may be, as distinct from the overemphasis of the stereotype. This helps to account for the fact that there have always, in every society, been men who are seen as "feminine" and women who are seen as "masculine" when judged by the stereotypes of their culture. The more rigid the cultural views on what constitutes "true" masculinity or femininity, the harder the lot of those who are perceived as being too much like the other sex.

PSYCHOLOGICAL THEORIES OF HOW THEY DIFFER

The question as to what is inborn and what is acquired is extraordinarily difficult. Certainly *nothing* is innate in the precise form in which we see it in adults, since by that time any biological predispositions have been continuously interacting with the socializing forces of the culture into which the person was born. A further complication is that researchers attempting to clarify the issue are themselves women (or men) who have been socialized in a particular way and therefore probably have some blind spots about the matter. In short, true scientific objectivity about the ultimate differences between men and women may be impossible at this time, since we are all struggling with the stifling influence of old stereotypes. Nevertheless, some light is better than none, and we do not have to remain the victims of old prejudices. Important work has been done, and more is under way.

In the early part of this century Sigmund Freud, the founder of psychoanalysis, followed ancient practice and decided that what he found in *men* constituted a standard for *all* human beings. (I say "ancient" because the Greeks believed that women had fewer teeth than men and were therefore inferior. After all, the number of teeth men had was clearly the *right* number!) Since women were observably different, there was obviously something wrong with them, poor things. Their strivings for independence were perceived as "penis envy," and their frequently heroic willingness to endure personal distress for the sake of maintaining relationships was interpreted as "masochism." A woman's baby was said to have the unconscious significance of a substitute for the missing penis! Of course this was not made up out of thin air. Psychoanalysis does uncover such ideas in some neurotic women. But the early analysts, nearly all of whom were male, failed to find any corresponding envy of women— uterus and breast envy, for instance—in neurotic men, or to interpret their relative lack of concern for relationships as pathological in any way. Yet to many psychiatrists not blinded by the prejudice of male supremacy these dynamics in some men are obvious. I wonder how many cases of this sort we would see in persons of either sex if our culture did not make women feel inferior or men feel ashamed of their supposedly feminine tendencies. (My criticism of this aspect of Freud's thought is not intended to minimize the inestimable contribution he made to the better understanding of human suffering. Without his work, we would still be in the psychological Dark Ages.)

One of Freud's early followers, Carl Jung, took a different view. More than sixty years ago he claimed that the *masculine principle* and the *feminine principle* were separate and of equal importance. Therefore, to understand the psychology of women it was necessary to study them in their own terms. He also discovered that the psyche of every person contained elements of both principles. Those qualities which are included in the feminine principle manifest consciously in women but through the unconscious in men, where they are referred to as the *anima*. The masculine principle manifests consciously in men, but in women it is expressed through the unconscious as *animus*. This contrasexual unconscious component may be almost completely suppressed. Or it may operate behind the scenes in ways that can be very confusing. In mature people it is accepted, reasonably well understood, and integrated into their total psychological economy.

From his research in history, mythology, and the customs of other cultures, Jung concluded that these two principles form part of the given structure of the human psyche—perhaps of the universe. This parallels the Oriental idea that divides everything there is into *yang* (masculine) and *yin* (feminine), which should always be in balance, supporting and complementing one another. Jung came to the same conclusion. A remnant of such ideas in the West can be found in the fact that most languages (English being one of the exceptions) assign a gender to every noun. At one time, masculine or feminine qualities were attributed to everything there is! This level of meaning for the terms "masculine" and "feminine" is highly symbolic and, as applied to actual men and women, refers *only* to the inborn tendency to develop the kind of psychic structure described above, a psychological genetics, so to speak. Jung used the word "archetypal" to describe this basic level. In individuals, the actual forms this takes depend on the specific circumstances of each person's development, including the customs of the person's native culture.

When speaking of the differences between men and women, we are concerned with three levels, which it is very important to keep straight. The first is the *symbolic* or *archetypal* level, referred to above. The second is the *cultural* and *psychological* level. The third is the *biological*, referring only to the body. The archetypal level is intangible—we never see it directly, only its effects. This basic predisposition of the human psyche is just raw material. Like every other aspect of human personhood, it depends on its interaction with the environment for the precise form it will take, and that is where cultural factors enter the picture. It is also where the specific circumstances of each person's upbringing have their effect. A good analogy is to the genetic coding in every human body, which determines that it will have the characteristic, recognizable human form, including whether it will be male or female. But how each human body develops in exact detail depends not only on its original genetic endowment but on nutrition, exercise, health or illness, and many other factors.

In summary, when we speak of someone being *male* or *female*, we are merely referring to an obvious physical fact. But when we speak of *masculine* or *feminine* personality characteristics or behavior, we are talking about something that has many different variations, something that results from the exceedingly complex interaction between a given archetypal predisposition and the total environment of the individual, including the rest of the person's own personality, conscious and unconscious.

Thus the masculine principle and feminine principle, as manifested in men and women, refer to *qualities of consciousness*, which *both* men and women have. (Since confusion on this point is likely, I must emphasize that this normal androgyny of the psyche does *not* predispose people to homosexuality or bisexuality. Those conditions have other causes, beyond the scope of this book.) The aspects of the principles, and the particular configuration they take in individuals, depend on cultural and psychological factors during development. The trick is to tell the difference: what is basic and therefore modifiable only with difficulty, if at all, and what is the accumulated result of social forces.

So far, psychological research suggests that the real differences are far more subtle than the old stereotypes would suggest. For example, a man or a woman may be a person of high principles or may be a scoundrel. That basic moral disposition has nothing to do with sex. But the way in which moral principles are conceptualized, the methods chosen to implement them, the circumstances that are perceived as problematic—all those do vary between men and women. It is a matter of style, emphasis, proportion, and order of priority naturally assigned to things.

To put it another way, even when equally interested in something, men and women seem to look at it differently. And that suggests an analogy which may give a rough idea. Consider the human eye. We have two types of vision, macular and peripheral. The first is what we use when we need to *focus* closely on something in order to see precise details. Peripheral vision shows the larger *context* in which the object we are scrutinizing is situated. Peripheral vision is also more sensitive to faint light sources than macular vision, but what is seen is blurred. It would be foolish to claim that one kind of vision is "better" than the other, since without both we cannot see properly. Not only that, for many purposes we really need to use both simultaneously. Without the context we could not know what we were looking at. Without the focus we could not see anything clearly.

Those are the two key words to give the essence of the principles as described by Jung and his followers: *focus* corresponds to the masculine principle and *context* to the feminine. In terms of human behavior this means that men on the whole tend to be analytic—to take things or ideas apart in order to examine the parts more closely. Carol Gilligan's work, referred to in the last chapter, confirms this as she describes the differences between the ways men and women approach moral dilemmas. Men analyze the problem, figure out its parts, then choose among them. Women prefer not to do that. They try to keep all issues in view simultaneously, even when that makes it difficult or impossible to choose one "right" answer. This confirms Jung's view of women as having a more inclusive style than men. Men therefore tend to be goal-oriented, while women are more oriented to situations.

Correlated with this is the greater interest men seem to have in things *as they are in themselves.* This is not to say that women are never materialistic, but that women's interest in things, *as things,* is likely to be subsidiary to the role they play in their relationships with people or in the way they value themselves. Research on infants confirms this, as from birth girls respond faster to human contact, at first being relatively uninterested in inanimate objects. Boys, on the other hand, are interested in things from the start.

The value of just *being* is more likely to be appreciated by women, while men are more likely to value *doing* something. Most mothers find boys more active than girls, less willing just to be with people and enjoy their company. Again, this is confirmed by research. More than 90 percent of the children diagnosed as "hyperactive" are boys, but it turns out that with few exceptions the way they are behaving is perfectly normal *for boys,* but not for girls. Just sitting and reading or listening drives them up a wall. This is probably related to the fact that at about eighteen months boys show a kind and degree of aggressiveness that is absent in girls. While some of this remains as a tendency to fight—a tendency unfortunately encouraged by many parents—much of it gets diverted into other active channels. This is not to say women and girls are not active. Of course they are, and indeed the world would grind to a halt if they were not. But the factors that underlie their behavior are different, and the activity itself is usually carried out in a different style.

Jung expressed the contrast in the two styles by saying that *perfection* is a masculine ideal, while woman inclines by nature to *completeness.* But perfection is only achievable on paper, so this leads to a tendency for men to be more theoretical and abstract than women. Completeness, on the other hand, requires attention to detail and therefore leads women to attend to the particular and the concrete.

I am sure that readers have thought of exceptions to nearly every statement in the preceding descriptions, and some may even have wondered whether I am not simply reinforcing some of the old stereotypes. Here I remind you of what I said earlier in this chapter, that *the sexual component of identity is only one of many others. In particular individuals, or in special circumstances, it may be the least important determinant of behavior.* Just because we find a *tendency* to respond in a certain way there is no implication that the person cannot respond in other ways when these are appropriate. And it is also important to remember that we are actually talking about *qualities of consciousness* that both men and women have. Under the influence of sexual stereotyping, the motivation and the encouragement for both men and women to develop and use their alternate faculties have usually been absent.

WOMEN'S NEGLECTED QUALITIES

The net effect of the combination of patriarchy and our stereotypes is that men overestimate themselves while women underestimate themselves. Their natural qualities have been disparaged, and their best talents given inferior labels. Even for very "liberated" women, it takes effort to realize that the single-minded, *focused*, logically carried-out pursuit of a goal is not "better" than a more diffuse and inclusive approach. For example, it used to be said—in some places still is—that women are illogical because they change their minds a lot, can't stick to the subject, and get emotional when they should be keeping a cool head. Who wants a person like that in a business meeting? That's no way to go about making important decisions!

Such an assessment looks at things from the point of view of masculine values. Women behave differently from men, so they must be off base. But let's turn that around. We mustn't forget that the words we choose to describe behavior are not objective but reflect a value judgment we have already made. For example, the difference between "stubborn" and "persistent" is in the mind of the observer, not in the behavior itself. Instead of describing women negatively as flighty, unable to stick to the subject, and overemotional, we can choose positive terms for the same behavior. No matter what aspect of a problem is under discussion, women immediately see how that relates to the total context and are flexible enough to suggest changes of plan based on those insights. Not only that, they perceive at once what effect the proposals will have on the feelings (and therefore the performance) of the people involved. Who can do without somebody like that in a business meeting? It would be foolish to make important decisions without that perspective!

Women's special strengths have not been identified and developed in terms that clarify their value to all human activities. Until very recently, even feminists have put most of their efforts into getting women admitted to jobs hitherto closed to them, emphasizing that women are "just as good as" men. In terms of being able to acquire the technical proficiency required to perform any tasks as well as men (except those depending primarily on physical strength), this is certainly true. But it overlooks the fact that women have a different *style* from men, a style which is not "better than" men's style but which is complementary and carries assets that the world sorely needs.

To the extent that women carry the burden of thinking

they always ought to be able to function naturally in the masculine mode, they are wasting their energy and adding to whatever insecurities or feelings of inferiority they may already have. Instead of asking themselves "Who am I?" they waste time and energy trying to figure out "Who should I be?"

WOMEN'S RESPONSE TO MALE PRIVILEGE

Another problem that gets in the way of women knowing who they really are relates to their perception of men as enjoying a privileged position in society. If they believe that men are entitled to that position, they may play follow-the-leader without examining closely whether what they are asked to follow really suits them or agrees with their own values. They may raise occasional objections, but it is all too easy for such women to decide they were wrong even when their deepest intuitions make them uneasy. The idea that their own views might be best is so difficult for them that when it comes to a real showdown they tend to back off.

Other women, also noticing men's privilege, are jealous of it. They think that all they want is what the men have, and set out to compete with them on their own terms in order to get it. Any suggestion that their true needs and wishes might be different is vigorously rejected because they see it as relegating them to inferior status. When their own feminine style tries to surface, they quickly suppress it, seeing it only as a hindering weakness.

At least indirectly, both these problems—lack of awareness of their own special strengths, and response to men's privilege—derive from women's natural tendency to experience themselves in terms of their primary concern for relationships. But even women who are aware of their strengths and who are neither competitive nor compliant have difficulties directly traceable to that concern. I have often lectured about what women have to offer, describing their special assets. Every time in the question period some woman says, "That sounds wonderful, but how can we get men to let us do those things?" I reply, "You are an adult, you do not need permission." The plaintive response is, "Yes, but what if he gets angry? What do I do then?" Such women are expressing their deep belief that a breach of relationship *must* be avoided, even if this means forgoing something truly important to themselves. Rather than risk anything of the sort, many women hide even from themselves who they really are and what they really want. Of course most of them can be assertive about minor issues, even if it means some temporary unpleasantness. But a major issue, one that might provoke a serious breach, is much harder— often impossible. Nor do women only respond like this when men are involved. They do it with each other as well.

We have reviewed some of the reasons why it is truly hard work for women to explore the full extent of their own personal identity. But it is extremely important, for everyone's sake, that they learn to do it. The next chapter will explain just why that is so.

REFERENCES

Schlafly, Phyllis, *The Power of the Positive Woman.* Arlington House, 1977. Chapter III, pp. 134–148.

If you want to read more about the differences between men and women, you may find the following books helpful.

Barnhouse, Ruth Tiffany, and Holmes, Urban T. (eds.), *Male and Female, Christian Approaches to Sexuality.* Seabury Press, 1976.

Miller, Jean Baker, *Toward a New Psychology of Women.* Beacon Press, 1977. This excellent book discusses the subject from a non-Jungian point of view. Dr. Miller uses her extensive psychiatric experience to correct old errors, while retaining an essentially Freudian perspective.

The following six books give a good understanding of Jung's view of masculine and feminine and how they interact. The first four are easy to read. The last two go into much more detail but are still intended for the general reader.

Claremont De Castillejo, Irene, *Knowing Woman: A Feminine Psychology.* G. P. Putnam's Sons, 1973. Also available in paperback as a Harper Torchbook. This is the simplest exposition of the Jungian point of view.

Jung, Emma, *Animus and Anima.* Spring Publications, 1972. This very readable little book was written over forty years ago by Carl Jung's wife.

Sanford, John, *The Invisible Partners.* Paulist Press, 1980. This explains how the masculine and feminine interact, consciously and unconsciously. It has useful suggestions on how to become more aware and more effective in actual relationships.

Ulanov, Ann Belford, *Receiving Woman.* Westminster Press, 1981. This excellent book goes into more detail, including some theological reflections.

Harding, Esther M., *Woman's Mysteries.* Bantam Books, 1973. This was written nearly fifty years ago and is therefore addressed to a different stage of feminism than we are now in. It deals extensively with ancient mythologies and interprets those for modern women.

Ulanov, Ann Belford, *The Feminine in Jungian Psychology and Christian Theology.* Northwestern University Press, 1971. This is the best and most extensive treatment of the subject I have ever seen. It is full of contemporary examples and will be illuminating to all who read it.

CHAPTER 4

Why Is Women's Identity Important to Everybody?

The crucial balance between the values of individualism and those of community can no longer be maintained by assigning one half to men and the other half to women. An old proverb says, "The hand that rocks the cradle rules the world." In our time that is heard as a cynical device to keep women in their place. But until after World War I to say that a man was devoted to his mother and valued her advice was a strong character reference. Now such statements would be seen as telling us about his hang-ups and casting doubt on his general reliability. Most women are so blinded by recent legal gains that they do not notice they have lost ground spiritually and emotionally. The patriarchal system worked for the benefit of all when, and *only* when, "women's sphere," however that was defined, had equal stature and dignity with that of men. The world is now suffering from a runaway development of the masculine principle, with a corresponding atrophy of feminine values. Much of this is men's fault. But women have a great share in the responsibility for this deplorable fact, importantly caused by their failure to know and trust *who they are in themselves.*

HOW WOMEN PERPETUATE THE IMBALANCE

Much of men's resistance to women's liberation is because they fear it will limit their freedom to pursue their own individual ends. They will have to start carrying more of the responsibility for relationship and community. Some men are aware of this resistance, but I cannot emphasize too strongly that for the great majority of them it is present only as an inarticulate sense that women are somehow in the way. They may even be ashamed of the feeling.

The new attitude toward women really is in men's way. For instance, in the old days a man could announce to his wife, "We are moving to Chicago in six weeks." Sometimes a courteous man would say, "I have had a good offer in Chicago. What would you think of moving there?" But he could think to himself what a fine fellow he was to consult her. There are now many men who have reached that stage—but *only* that stage. Should such a man's wife raise adamant objections, he usually feels aggrieved. He was nice to her, why isn't she being nice to him and allowing herself to be convinced? What is now required is for him to know that it shouldn't even occur to him not to consult her, and that if the move does get made, it must be with her free consent. That change in attitude is doubly difficult, since he is made to feel guilty about behavior which his father and grandfather took for granted. No wonder many men regret the "good old days" and feel their ancient liberties encroached on.

This difficulty is complicated by those women who see liberation mainly in terms of getting to do what men have always done and who are trying to do it the same way. Many are unable to carry this program through. But even the attempt is dangerous to society, because it aggravates the existing overemphasis on individualistic striving at the expense of the values of communal cooperation. It also leaves men feeling that feminism is only trying to take things away from them. What they need to realize is that at its best feminism will give them something they lack.

A typical feminist mistake is the adamant opposition to the long tradition of women volunteers. The argument goes that only money gives work any value in the eyes of society and that the esteem in which a person is held is directly related to earning power. To work for nothing is to invite contempt, therefore women should be paid for all the work they do. But volunteer work expresses, as few other activities do, the ideal of care for the needs of the entire community, not just the pleasure or advantage of individuals fortunate enough to be able to take care of themselves. Although most volunteers are women, many men also do such work for the Boy Scouts and many other organizations. The feminist attitude devalues that too. Yet where would we all be without it? Instead of putting women down for "volunteerism," we should encourage more men to follow their example.

Other ways women contribute to the imbalance relate to issues discussed in the last chapter. Women are less concerned with great general theories than they are with specific situations involving them. As we saw, they frequently compromise their own beliefs and values—even fail to discover what those are—for the sake of preserving their relationships. Some of the women who ask "But how do we get them to let us do those things?" have important jobs in business or the professions. They manage by means of graceful compromise, by not rocking the boat. Often they secure the approval of an important man in the organization who will back them up when they wish to propose something controversial. Other indirect, even devious and manipulative tactics may be used. Since this way of doing things comes so naturally to women, they usually do not realize that self-determined individuals function differently. Self-determined people who want to get something done practice the usual social graces, but *keeping everybody happy is not the bottom line*! Both at home and on the job, women far too often misapply their "mothering" tendencies and cater inappropriately to the "fragile male ego."

There are many respects in which men *are* more fragile than women. Women are more resilient, both physically and emotionally, and they cope with stress significantly better. The patriarchal attitude allows women to admit that they are in trouble, weak, or frightened, and admitting a problem is the indispensable first step to solving it. In this respect women are more realistic than men. The difference between male and female bodies is relevant here. From the start a woman must learn to be in a cooperative relationship with her body, since it undergoes processes—such as menstruation and childbearing—over which she has little or no control, and because she is relatively weak physically. Men, being stronger, tend to treat their bodies like a fancy power tool with which they can subdue the environment. Since we have long outgrown the time when brute force was necessary to deal with a hostile environment, this attitude has outlived its usefulness as a basic principle of behavior. Worse, in modern conditions it can easily turn antisocial. And yet we continue to associate it with manhood.

Let me give an example. I teach a course in Marriage and Family to students, nearly all of whom are in their last year of theological seminary. There are more men than women in the class, but they have been very well trained. None of them would think of using any sexist language. But recently we did a role-play. A woman, played by a woman student, was taking a problem to her pastor, played by a male student. She was concerned about her fifteen-year-old son, who she feared was on the

road to juvenile delinquency. Her husband said she was
turning him into a sissy and insisted that there was
nothing wrong with the boy's outbreaks of violence,
dangerous games, and vandalism. There was serious
trouble not only between herself and her son but also
with her husband. She was asking her pastor how to
handle the problem.

The way that role-play developed, supplemented by
the later discussion, made clear that nearly all the men in
the room felt in their gut that the hypothetical husband
was right. Boys will be boys. To grow into men they must
be tough, rough, competitive, they must fight, dominate
others, and at least go through a period of showing contempt for women. Many of the men students knew in-
tellectually that such ideas need modification, but they
could not imagine any other way to bring up a boy so that
he would turn out to be a "real man." Even worse was the
fact that none of the women could figure out what to do
without the husband's cooperative approval! Yet they
were all agreed that the boy's behavior should not go
unchecked.

When women go along with things they do not believe
are right, they are simultaneously bolstering the patriarchy and catering to the "fragile male ego." Logical
analysis shows that these two goals are really incompat-
ible. If men are that fragile, what are they doing in
charge? The result of such behavior by women is to allow
men to live in a fantasy world, imagining themselves to
be stronger (not just physically) than they really are. This
is bad for everybody.

I once heard a woman in her fifties who had been a
church secretary in the same parish for over twenty years
talk about her experiences. At first she insisted that traditional ways were best and seemed to agree that men
ought to run things. But as she gained confidence, we
gradually heard the true story. During those twenty years,

one minister had a messy affair with a woman in the congregation and left abruptly. The secretary essentially ran the church until a new minister was found. He became a chronic alcoholic—but the secretary always covered up for him. He finally left, and few suspected his incompetence because she had managed everything so well. A third was just out of seminary and tried to hide his inexperience behind an extremely authoritarian manner, frequently giving orders that made no sense. She tactfully covered for him, changing his orders behind his back—but as though he himself had told her to do so. By the end of her story, it was clear that she thought they were all fools and that the church would have collapsed without her. But she completely failed to see that she had contributed to the foolishness by allowing it to go undetected by others.

Doing the dirty work behind the scenes while helping men to look good no matter what is one of woman's classic roles. *It is a terrible mistake.* In such a setup men do not have to bear the real consequences of their behavior—in fact, they do not even see their behavior for what it is. Women treat them as adolescents, encouraging their good points and tactfully passing over their faults. It may sometimes be necessary for boys going through the agonizing uncertainties of the transition from childhood to adulthood to be mothered in that way. But women tend to do it too much and too long. What they forget is that adolescent males have a treacherous tendency to bite the hand that feeds them. Overprotective women are setting themselves up to be exploited or worse, since they make handy scapegoats if anything goes wrong.

This prevents men from growing up, from ever facing the full consequences of their "look, Ma, no hands!" approach to life. They persist in adolescent behavior, which is characterized by mistaking recklessness for courage, bullying for bravery. They confuse getting their own way with independence, and the aggressive instinct is imperfectly civilized.

THE MASCULINE PRINCIPLE
IS DANGEROUS BY ITSELF!

In some cases aggression and sexuality are seriously entangled. The complaint about movies and television is that there is too much sex and violence, almost as though it were one word, "sexandviolence." Most people think these are different things, but they are not. Consider our slang: the same word "screw" (or its cruder synonym), is used for the sex act and to express anger ("screw you!") or exploitation ("I've been screwed!"). This is *not* the case in all cultures! There is a natural connection between the sexual and aggressive instincts in the beginning, at least in males. Some strong initiative is necessary for sexual success. But remember what I said earlier about aggression: It does not have to be hostile but can be rechanneled into constructive activity. Unfortunately, that lesson does not always get learned. It is often asserted that rape is not a sexual crime but a violent one. While true in a way, that overlooks the connection between sex and aggression. Men who have been sexually frustrated often respond by picking a fight. And if a man is feeling violent, he can often be seduced out of it.

Even when there is no actual violence, people's sexual attitudes and their attitudes to power are connected. Henry Kissinger once said, "Power is the ultimate aphrodisiac" (and thereby went to the top of the list of men I wouldn't want my daughter to go out with). Some women play up to men who have that attitude because they feel powerless themselves, and so the only way they see to get power is vicariously, through association with a powerful man.

This kind of power is dangerous. It does not relate to

other people with care and respect, but as pawns to be manipulated in the ever-escalating game of personal aggrandizement. It has a corrupting effect on character, best described by the great eighteenth-century British statesman Edmund Burke: "Power gradually extirpates from the mind every humane and gentle virtue." This has been demonstrated in the twentieth century to an extent Burke would never have imagined possible. Hitler's immature lust for power killed six million Jews. But that pales into insignificance when we hear that some of our own elected officials and high-ranking military men are talking about a hundred and twenty million "acceptable" civilian deaths in a nuclear war. Arguments justifying this stance boil down to two premises: We must be stronger than they are, and you can't trust them. That is the mindset of teenage males in rival gangs in the slums of New York. When we see it on that scale we recognize its vicious immaturity. It is incomparably worse when used to "justify" the terrible risk of annihilating the human family.

Father Arnold, a Roman Catholic priest, says:

> The historical catastrophes of our time can be traced back to the predominance of the active, self-reliant male principle in our civilization and the corresponding atrophying of the feminine principle. . . . This world without women is more the world of adolescents than the world of men. It is in the last analysis a world of men on their own, . . . hardened by their own pride, no longer aware of sin or in need of grace. It is a world which has shaken off all transcendental ties . . . it is without God.

And some years ago William Thompson, a former history professor at Massachusetts Institute of Technology, wrote a scathing book about the evils of runaway technology, which he described as an exaggerated, unbalanced de-

velopment of immature masculine values culminating in
the rape of Mother Earth and possibly in the murder of
all of her children. More recently, Lewis Thomas, author
of *The Lives of a Cell*, suggested that for the next hundred
years only women should be allowed to vote. Men have
made a mess of things, and perhaps women's more caring
nature could prevent us from destroying ourselves. It
would be a mistake to take that suggestion literally, since
women would probably make a mess of things too. But it
would be a different kind of mess. A statement made by
O. S. Fowler in the nineteenth century is better: "What
women do not help do is miserably done; what they may
not do, should not *be* done. ... Mutuality in *all* things,
isolation in none, that is the natural law." Amen! These
men all see that our whole culture is out of balance
because the feminine principle has been relegated to an
inferior position.

We can move from the terrible example of nuclear
annihilation to the familiar if somewhat ridiculous one of
what happens when a man is going somewhere and gets
lost. Does he promptly stop at the nearest gas station to
ask directions? Not on your life. Most men will drive
around for ages, insisting that they can find the way
without help and taking as a personal affront any suggestion that to get directions would be more efficient.

Why are they so silly? Because our stereotypes have
damaged not just women but men also. Usually they are
socialized to believe that a "real man" is always in control, always knows what's going on, never lets his feelings interfere with "realistic" decisions, can handle any
situation—and must pretend he can even if he knows
better. Since women are socialized entirely differently,
they cannot imagine the degree to which this need to be
in control is associated with a man's central sense of
identity *as a man*. When his control is threatened, so is
his virility. Men can accept hierarchical arrangements,

particularly those which afford them the opportunity to climb the ladder to greater success. They can accept losing an argument or a fight on the principle of "May the better man win." But *voluntary* abdication of control is another matter.

This is why it is so hard for most men to admit illness, either physical or mental. This is why men so frequently refuse the plea of their unhappy wives that a marriage counselor should be consulted: the man cannot tolerate the idea of a problem he cannot solve himself—it makes him feel less than a man. Given the obvious fragility of each human being, and the fact that not one of us could survive for long without the help and cooperation of others, such attitudes are completely unrealistic. To raise a boy with the idea that he can be in charge all the time, and that unless he is, he is not a "real man," is to invite both personal and social disaster.

This puts men in an intolerable position of constant pretense, which is one of the primary sources of ulcers, heart attacks, high blood pressure, and other stress diseases. We are used to hearing about the oppression of women. But what is the most extreme form of oppression? It kills you. And men in our culture die, on the average, five to ten years before women, mostly because we have raised them to think they are not supposed to have problems. On the social level, men are encouraged to be destructively competitive and to project all their own faults and weaknesses onto others. This leads to a generally adversarial approach to life. It also leads to a preoccupation with power, narrowly and badly defined as power *over* other people. How else can one explain such idiocies as months of discussion by subordinates over who should sit where at the conference table before peace talks between opposing nations can even get started? It has been truly said that if you seek power, all you really get is vanity.

THE SOLUTION: MUTUAL RESPECT
AND APPRECIATION

None of what has been said so far should be misinterpreted to mean that the feminine principle in general (much less any woman in particular) is superior to the masculine principle. What Father Arnold describes as the "active, self-reliant male principle" is absolutely essential to human growth. Without it we would still be in the Stone Age. It cannot be emphasized too strongly that what is required is a *balance* between the masculine and feminine principles. In every situation Carol Gilligan's questions need to be asked. We already know the answer to "What does he see that she does not?" but the answer to the other question, "What does *she* see that *he* does not?" also needs to be sought, found, and applied.

For the derivatives of both principles to be applied appropriately to life's challenges, there must be a relation of mutual respect between men and women. They must learn to know and cherish the difference in their outlooks, but also to recognize and cultivate the similarities of their common humanity. As human beings they will have common goals. As men and women they may differ considerably in the style and technique of approaching those goals. And they must learn not to let those differences be a source of contention but rather to appreciate the fullness of their complementarity. Under such circumstances, what men and women can do together is much more than the sum of what they can do separately. This is what Prof. Fowler meant when he said, "Mutuality in all things, isolation in none, that is the natural law."

At the present state of human evolution there are still times when the "macho" approach to problems is needed.

Because they are trying so hard to overturn that philosophy's dominance, it is often hard for women to admit this. It is also hard for men, even well-meaning ones, to give up being "macho" when it is not appropriate. But many are working hard at it—a task that needs the intelligent support of their wives and women friends. An example from contemporary fiction will show what I mean and is particularly important since it comes from the pen of a man.

Robert B. Parker, formerly an English professor at Northeastern University and a veteran of the Korean War, now writes suspense stories. The detective hero of his series is Spenser, who is fanatic about physical fitness, independence, bravery—but also about honor and living strictly by his own code. The books are written in the first person, with Spenser himself as the narrator. In the third novel of the series, *Mortal Stakes*, Marty, a baseball pitcher for the Red Sox, and his wife, Linda, are in trouble. Spenser has been hired by the team manager for another reason, and in the course of his investigation he discovers that Marty and Linda are being blackmailed— and he also knows why and decides to rescue them. At first Marty is extremely angry that an outsider knows anything about their private affairs, because he—in his own way just as "macho" as Spenser—thinks he should handle his own family troubles. The following dialogue illustrates the attitude of the men but also the intelligent intervention of Linda *and* the fact that Marty respects the wisdom of her approach. Marty has just expressed his desire to beat Spenser up. Spenser replies:

> "Marty, you are the third person this morning who has offered to disassemble my body. You are also the third in order of probable success. I can't throw a baseball like you can, but the odds are very good that I could put you in the hospital before you ever

got a hand on me." I was getting sick of people
yelling at me. . . .

Linda Rabb let go of his arm and came around in
front of him and put both her arms around his waist.
"Stop it, Marty. Both of you grow up. This isn't a
playground where you little boys can prove to each
other how tough you are. This is our home and our
future and little Marty and our life. You can't handle
every problem as if it were an arm-wrestling con-
test." . . .

"But, Jesus Christ, Linda, a man's gotta—"

She screamed at him, the voice muffled against
his chest. "Shut up. Just shut up about a man's
gotta." . . .

Rabb put his arms around his wife and rubbed the
top of her head with his chin.

"I don't know," he said. "I don't know what in
hell to do."

"Me either," I said. "But if you'd sit down, maybe
we could figure something out." (Robert B. Parker,
Mortal Stakes, p. 142)

The success of this scene depends on two things. First,
the men truly respect the woman's competence and are
willing to accept suggestions that make sense, *even when
these suggestions go against their own spontaneous style.*
Second, the woman knows who she is and what her
values are, she has confidence in them, and she feels
absolutely no need to defer to men when she thinks they
are wrong; therefore, when she speaks, there is no apol-
ogy, no hint that were he to disagree she would back
down. In addition she correctly recognizes that her feelings are a vital part of the situation and is neither ashamed
nor embarrassed to cry while making her point. If she had
not had this kind of firm self-confidence, she would
probably not have been heeded. It comes down to the old
adage—you can't sell a product you don't believe in
yourself.

Another scene from the same book illustrates this process in reverse, a woman accepting the macho approach to a problem, recognizing that her own way would not have had a chance. Spenser has shot and killed two underworld criminals and, feeling very shaken, goes to visit his lady, Susan, who is a guidance counselor. He doesn't think this out—he just goes, intuitively sensing that he really needs a mature feminine perspective on what has happened and also (as those of you who read the book will see) that he needs to confess *to a woman.*

> "I set them up," I said. "I got them up there to kill them."
> "Yes, and you walked in on them from the front, two of them to one of you, like a John Wayne movie. How many men do you think would have done that?
> . . .
> "You'd have had to kill them," Susan said. "Sometime. Now it's done. What does it matter how?"
> "That's the part that does matter. How. It's the only part that matters."

Here Susan is doing the typical feminine thing—considering the particulars of the immediate situation, while he, again typically, is concerned about the theoretical aspects. She encourages him to explain:

> "Honor?" Susan said.
> "Yeah," I said. . . .
> "I'm not making fun," Susan said, "but aren't you older and wiser than that?"

Spenser says that both he and Marty are suffering because their "code" didn't work. When Susan asks whether the code couldn't be adjusted, he replies:

> "Then it's not a code anymore. See, being a person is kind of a random and arbitrary business. You may have noticed that. And you need to believe in something to keep it from being too random and

> arbitrary to handle. . . . So you accept some system
> of order, and you stick to it. For Rabb it's playing
> ball. You give it all you got and you play hurt and
> you don't complain and so on and if you're good you
> win and the better you are the more you win so the
> more you win the more you prove you're good. But
> for Rabb it's also taking care of the wife and kid, and
> the two systems came into conflict. He couldn't be
> true to both. And now he's compromised and he'll
> never have the same sense of self he had before."

This passage illustrates well the masculine concern with
perfection. Spenser is upset because he cannot *perfectly*
meet two conflicting requirements of his code.

> "And," Susan said, "two moral imperatives in
> your system are never to allow innocents to be
> victimized and never to kill people except involun-
> tarily. Perhaps the words aren't quite the right ones,
> but that's the idea, isn't it? . . . And this time you
> couldn't obey both those imperatives. You had to
> violate one."
> I nodded again.
> "I understand," she said. . . . "I can't make it
> better."

She knows she can't resolve this anxiety over perfection
for him, if only because that is not the aspect of the
situation she finds most compelling. But she does not
assault him with her different viewpoint, she simply
acknowledges that his terms are not hers. Susan finally
says to him:

> "Spenser, . . . you are a classic case for the femi-
> nist movement. A captive of the male mystique, and
> all that. And I want to say, for God's sake, you fool,
> outgrow all that Hemingwayesque nonsense. And
> yet . . ." She leaned her head against my shoulder as
> she spoke. "And yet I'm not sure you're wrong. I'm
> not sure but what you are exactly what you ought to

be. What I am sure of is I'd care for you less if killing
those people didn't bother you." (Pp. 187–190)

Now she finally expresses her feminine viewpoint but is
mature enough to recognize that it is not the only possible way in all circumstances.

Her confidence in herself makes it possible for her to
be gentle and helpful in this shocking situation. If she
were not sure of her own values and had not already
communicated that sureness to him, he probably would
not have turned to her in the first place, much less been
able to profit by the encounter.

The essential point is that women who *do* know who
they are in themselves, and are consciously proud of their
particular gifts, knowing how and when to exercise them
for the benefit of all, are in a position to be effective in
redressing the imbalance between the masculine and
feminine principles in all aspects of life. This does not
mean that they all have to work outside the home, as has
sometimes been claimed. Linda was a housewife, Susan
a professional woman. What it does mean is that each
woman, on the basis of her understanding of who she is
in herself, chooses the role and life-style that suits her
best, whether that be "traditional" or "liberated." *True
liberation means having a choice.* And you can't choose,
in any meaningful sense of that term, unless you really
know who is doing the choosing.

When *every* member of the community is doing that
which uses her or his talents in a mature and effective
way rather than living in bondage to the expectations
imposed on us all by the stereotypes, men and women
can relate to one another on the basis of mutual respect
and appreciation. Too often that fails to happen, and so
exploitation of both sexes by one another is common.
Men's contempt for and exploitation of women has been
too well documented to need further comment. But

women have often taken a devious and manipulative revenge, trying to live out their own suppressed selves vicariously through men and children, to the extreme detriment of both. The common combination of overt submission to men and covert overprotective "mothering" of them is another way in which women damage not only themselves but also men. Women have significant responsibility for the current imbalance between the masculine and feminine principles that is endangering society at all levels. They will not be able to change their ingrained responses until they find and claim their true personal identity. Women must learn to do their own looking, *all* the time, at *all* problems affecting the human family, whether these are on the global, intermediate, or intimate scale. They must learn to have confidence in the validity of what they see, and to present and defend their vision with firm assertiveness. Then, and only then, will true liberation of the *whole* human community be possible.

REFERENCES

Parker, Robert B., *Mortal Stakes*. Dell Publishing Co., Inc., 1975. I strongly recommend the other books in this series, all of which (in addition to being fine whodunits) deal seriously with the man/woman relationship in totally contemporary terms.

Thompson, William Irwin, *At the Edge of History*. Harper Colophon, 1972. This book is especially interesting not only because it was written by a man but because it shows no trace of influence either from psychology or feminist ideology. He writes so well that it is almost impossible to put down.

CHAPTER 5

How Can Women Find
Their True Identity?

The answer to the question posed by this chapter has both theoretical and practical components. As already described in previous chapters, there are deeply rooted beliefs and ingrained patterns of response which, if not recognized and systematically dealt with, make it very difficult for women to find out who they are *in them-selves*. Some women are seriously affected by only one or two of these problematic issues, others are weighed down by all of them. Furthermore, their relative weight in any individual woman's life is not constant, varying not only with specific situations but with her general state of health, both physical and emotional.

The four most significant premises on which a woman's search for identity depends are these: She must recognize the advantages of the old ways and be willing either to give them up or to pay the price for retaining them; she must eradicate not only the conscious but the un-conscious belief in male supremacy; she must recognize the specifically feminine qualities of her consciousness and learn to value them appropriately; and she must realize that to find *herself* is not, and never can be, a betrayal of relationship with others.

The examples given in the following discussion will

show that in practice these issues are interrelated. Seldom, if ever, does one see a situation in which one is at work apart from the others. This naturally complicates the problems women have in trying to work through their difficulties.

ADVANTAGES OF THE OLD WAYS

In Chapter 2 we saw that women have given up varying degrees of freedom in order to get out of the corresponding amount of responsibility. In former times this did not make women feel ashamed of themselves, it was just the way things were. When *everyone* believed in male supremacy, it seemed reasonable for women's freedom *and* responsibility to be limited. Times have changed. Most women now want a great deal of freedom and believe that they are willing to shoulder the responsibility that goes with it.

But there is no getting away from the fact that what we consciously decide and how we actually function are often very different. Most people do not realize the degree to which the way they behave has almost nothing to do with their conscious beliefs but is the result of unconscious assimilation of family standards and the customs of their formative communities, such as church, school, and peer group. It is not enough to say to oneself, "I just don't believe that anymore and so am going to function differently." Far more accurate would be to say: "I am going to take the trouble to learn, little by little, to function differently, and I know it will be a long time before I have eradicated most of the old habits. And even after I have succeeded, I must not be surprised if from time to time doing things the new way makes me nervous."

For instance, a middle-aged woman, successful in her profession, got along very well with men until courtship began to surface. But the minute she sensed that a man's attentions had romantic overtones, she began to worry about whether or not she was pleasing him. If she invited him to dinner, instead of using her own judgment about what to serve, she tried to remember what dishes he chose in restaurants, never asking herself if it was something she liked, or how much trouble it would be to fix. If he consulted her about what movie they should go to, she would tell him to choose. If he was quiet during the evening, she wondered whether she had offended him. She did not approve of behaving like that, had no idea why she did it, and when she caught herself at it was not only furious but deeply ashamed. Furthermore, she was frightened by the loss of part of her identity—her independent standards of taste and conduct—that this behavior entailed. Fortunately she knew better than to imagine that her men friends were demanding this of her. After all, had they not been attracted by her usual independence of spirit they would hardly have approached her in the first place. She knew she was doing it to herself and was motivated to seek help.

Careful investigation showed that her *unconscious* response to being courted was that the man would make all decisions affecting their joint life, and so she must defer to his slightest wish. She was tired of always being in sole charge of her life, so turning everything over to someone else promised blessed relief from her lonely independence. Because she had conducted her adult life in opposition to the notion of male supremacy, she was ashamed of her wish, so she did not admit it, even to herself. Because the wish was unconscious, it influenced her behavior in a primitive way over which she had hardly any control. The essential first step, therefore, in overcoming her difficulty was to learn to recognize this motive.

Next we discovered the lingering effects of the belief

in male superiority that had prevailed in her family and childhood community. Because of those early experiences, her primary image of the man-woman relationship was one in which the man took the responsibility for everything, and so she responded automatically in those terms. She had no deeply ingrained model of responsibility *shared* with a man to fall back on. The solution of her problem consisted in helping her to develop such a model. This took many months of practical effort. At first she was in an agony of nervousness each time she tried it out, since she instinctively feared (even though she knew better) that to do so might threaten the developing relationship. She was gradually able to learn new techniques both for handling responsibility and for safeguarding relationships.

Some advantages of the old ways may be necessary in any well-functioning society. For example, because of their relative physical vulnerability, women need protection in many situations where men would not. These include childbearing and such things as working conditions that do not require women to go home alone late at night or to perform certain strenuous tasks. Too many women believe that in order to meet such needs they have to buy the whole old package. This is simply untrue. They do not need to give up *in principle* their freedom to be self-determining simply because there are some ways in which they are unable to be fully responsible for themselves. After all, there are things that only women can do, such as nurse babies. This is at least as basic to human survival as men's physical strength. But it would never occur to anyone to claim that because men cannot nurse babies they are automatically disqualified from taking other responsibilities!

If a woman knows that she doesn't want a lot of responsibility, and would enjoy a life where someone else carries most of that for her, she must be willing to give up a certain amount of freedom. This can work perfectly well *if it is a conscious decision,* but it will not work if she is trying to have her cake and eat it too. Nobody should make her feel inferior for having chosen that way of life. After all, not everyone finds full responsibility for all decisions temperamentally congenial.

However, this is *also true of men.* In a properly balanced society, men who naturally want to off-load some responsibility should not be made to feel guilty, much less "unmanly." Neither men nor women should need to pretend to have—or want—either more *or less* control than is natural to their temperament and circumstances and consistent with social harmony. People of both sexes become resentful, and behave in ways that are harmful not only to themselves but also to others, when they are forced by convention into a life-style that does not suit them. Much feminist rhetoric presents men's unquestioned power and control as altogether desirable and encourages women to claim it for themselves. But cases such as the one described above demonstrate that being in full charge is not always a bed of roses.

Women grappling with this issue and trying to find a workable compromise would do well to realize the strain men have been under, particularly since being in control has up to now been considered an indispensable part of essential masculine identity. Women have always had cultural permission to let somebody else be in charge, but men have not. Therefore, although not having as much control as they want, or as they feel able to take, may make women angry, it does not frighten them the way it frightens men. As we move together into the postpatriarchal era, women need to understand this point. The struggle to find better definitions of what it means to be a "real woman" or a "real man" is troublesome for *both* sexes.

THE LINGERING EFFECTS
OF MALE SUPREMACY

Many people imagine that the old idea of male superiority has been rooted out and there is no need to discuss
it further. They concede that it may still operate in the
consciousness of older women, or in country backwaters
which have not yet caught up with modern trends. Nothing could be farther from the truth. To be sure, most
women no longer *consciously* believe in the superiority
of men, but it is not easy to banish entirely something that
has governed social organization all over the world for
several thousand years. To make this point, I will describe a case that at first glance seems to contradict it.

A young lesbian came for help with severe depression
following an unhappy love affair. She had had disappoint-
ments in the past, but this one felt much worse. Her
former lover had decided that she was not a lesbian after
all and had made plans to marry. My patient was successful in her work. Nearly all her co-workers were women,
but her superiors were men. She conceded that some of
them were good at their jobs but said there was nothing
women could not do at least as well as men if only they
were not malevolently discriminated against. She attributed her own lack of promotion to this problem. Her
father had been an alcoholic wife-beater, and an uncle
had molested her in childhood. Her brothers were both
school dropouts, often in trouble with the law, but her
mother continued to behave as though they could do no
wrong. So it was not surprising that this young woman
was angry at men, perceiving them as bombastic, pre-
tentious, foolish, dangerous, unfeeling, and invariably
inclined to exploit women. This view made her lover's
desertion *to a man* unbearably painful.

But there was an odd contradiction. She was tough,

swore a lot, bragged a good deal about how intelligent and competent she was, smoked cigars, always wore pants—never dresses—and when she crossed her legs, she put one ankle up on the opposite knee. It was impossible to resist the conclusion that she was aping a certain kind of man in every possible way. After several months of work, we were able to discuss this. Why, if she thought so poorly of men, was she imitating them?

Without having admitted it to herself, she thought women were poor weak creatures. Only the masculine qualities included in her narrow version of the "macho" stereotype were admirable. She had met some kind, gentle men but dismissed them as "effeminate." She saw the world as a dog-eat-dog place, and dangerous, especially to women. So although she didn't *like* men, she envied their ability to compete in a fundamentally hostile environment, something her mother and the other women in her family had signally failed to do. Therefore, as she attempted to find her own place in the world, she rejected anything she saw as feminine in herself and used her very good mind to try to beat men at their own game. When her friend left her for a man, she had to face for the first time the possibility that she might not succeed in such a program, and this precipitated her serious depression. It shocked her to find that her militant feminism covered a deep concern about women's inadequacy and a strong belief in the overall superiority of the masculine. Not until these hidden prejudices were laid bare could she begin to build some real self-respect *as a woman.*

This example makes it plain that the idea of male supremacy is far more deep-seated than most people realize and can have serious effects on a woman's attitude to herself and to others, even when she has no idea that she is under its influence. This young woman's difficulties were compounded by her very negative image of femininity, owing to the emotional incompetence of her mother, who was unable to defend either herself or her daughter from male brutality. Most women are more fortunate in their life experiences. Nevertheless, the idea of male supremacy is in the very air we breathe from infancy, and I doubt if there are any women who do not have to deal with it one way or another at least occasionally.

Dealing with it is not really very difficult in most cases, *provided that its presence is admitted.* This is very hard for some women, since they can't believe that an idea they repudiate on intellectual or moral grounds could have any effect on their behavior and are often threatened by the suggestion that it might. But there is nothing shameful in recognizing that we are all products of our upbringing, and the path to maturity always involves the patient process of consciously facing its effects. Unless that is done, change is likely to be superficial, and one's progress, both private and public, can be disappointingly slow.

If male supremacy is believed in, the only way to improve the position of women is to claim that they are the same as men. The reason such a program is detrimental to women's true progress is that, as individual women try to accept it, their own tendency to believe in male superiority will be unconsciously reinforced, and they will be prevented from recognizing and using their specifically feminine strengths. Instead of learning to find out who they really are *as women*, they will continue to try to figure out what they ought to be like, using men's standards as a guide. Any problem with male supremacy may be aggravated when a woman has a valued relationship with a man. In such cases her concern to maintain the harmony of the relationship may prevent her from recognizing the ways in which that lingering belief is impeding her own process of self-discovery.

Very rarely one meets a woman who *really* believes

with all her heart and mind, consciously as well as un-consciously, that men are actually superior. Such a woman prefers, and gladly adopts, what to the rest of us is an outmoded life-style. However, she is sometimes angry with "those awful women's libbers" and may try to pre-vent "them" from encroaching on men's territory. At other times she is sweetly condescending, assuring other women that they will eventually regret venturing outside the charmed circle of male protection. One cannot help worrying about the fate of her daughters, who will cer-tainly live in a different world.

Finally, we need to recognize that the concept of the "fragile male ego" is derived from the notion of male supremacy. Men must come first, no matter what. Since much of their behavior so obviously contradicts any no-tion of their inherent superiority, the special fragility of their ego is postulated to account for the discrepancy. This explains why so many women take nearly full charge of their households or place of outside work, while con-tinuing to see the man's place as paramount. In such circumstances it is nearly impossible for women to value themselves appropriately.

VALUING FEMININE QUALITIES

In assessing their own gifts, women are frequently distracted by stereotypes. These say that men are logical, pragmatic, realistic, forceful, able to function without emotional distraction, and well fitted for leadership. Women are supposed not to understand machines or be good at figures. But they are considered intuitive, emo-tional, idealistic, and therefore not "realistic" about large issues. Now we all know men and women who do not fit these images, and yet they continue to govern our be-havior.

An amusing example will show what I mean. Several

years ago I was one of the speakers at a week-long conference on masculine/feminine issues. Many of the participants were married couples. They were very alert and prided themselves on their modern attitudes. As I explained the subtle effects of stereotypes, many felt that they already knew all that and had outgrown it in their own lives.

Toward the end of the conference a film was scheduled. The projector was not working properly. The sound was gravelly, and the picture twitched slightly. Several people got up and left, finding this poor quality annoying. When the young man in charge put in the second reel of the film, things were even worse. Finally he called out, "Does anyone know how to run this thing?" Instantly six or seven men appeared, none of whom knew any better than he did how to operate the machine. Finally, a woman who had been nearby from the start timidly offered to see what she could do. In seconds she had it working perfectly. The next morning, we learned that one of the women who had left early the evening before was in charge of the audiovisual department at the university where she worked, but it had never occurred to her to offer her services.

As demonstrated by this anecdote, the lingering effect of the stereotypes is an important cause of women's inability to recognize and claim their real gifts. As noted in Chapter 3, there are a great many components to every individual's total personality, and those qualities of consciousness that are directly or indirectly related to sex are by no means determinative. Many women have talents that the stereotypes associate only with men, but to the extent that the women continue to be influenced by those stereotypes, they are inhibited from developing their gifts for fear of being "unfeminine."

The obverse is also true. Many men have suffered because their intuitive, artistic gifts, coupled with low interest in things associated with the male stereotype, have been thought "unmanly." I have treated many a lawyer or accountant who would far rather have been an artist or a musician, but his father was horrified at the idea of any son of his taking up anything so "sissy"! People of both sexes need to figure out what sort of work they are really suited for, without worrying about whether what they choose is appropriate for their sex.

A related idea is that the things men do are important, but the things women do are not. That women are only good for taking care of kitchen, children, and church is an old claim, even though it ought to be obvious that there is nothing "only" about food, child care, and attention to the spiritual dimension. But the notion that women's work is trivial persists.

For instance, until World War I, women did not work in offices. That was "man's work." Even until World War II, most top secretarial positions were held by men. Since then, it has become "woman's work" and there is a tendency for everyone to despise it. Women's own disparagement of themselves has contributed significantly to this attitude. It is as though when women take over a field they assume there must have been something wrong with it or men would not have let that happen. Instead, they should consider the possibility that the real reason for the takeover is that women actually do the work better. In view of the fact that the entire economy would collapse in a matter of hours without good secretarial support, that explanation is far more logical.

If women have trouble recognizing their competence when it benefits others, they have even more difficulty when what they do is mainly for themselves. They mistakenly assume that is always selfish. Any lingering belief in male supremacy compounds this difficulty.

Until a woman has learned to appreciate her competence and to give up all tendency to defer to men just because they are men, it is very difficult for her to trust the distinctively feminine style that she may bring to the task at hand. But when she succeeds, she will never again take at face value any criticisms which, when properly analyzed, merely describe the fact that she is not approaching things the way a man would. Instead, she will see herself as an essential contributor to the task of restoring the balance between masculine and feminine in the world's affairs.

RELATIONSHIPS

Women's primary interest in maintaining relationships often prevents them from implementing the points made so far. It is also one of the most important things they have to contribute to our sadly unbalanced, dangerously hostile world. But women tend to fear that claiming their true identity might involve a degree of assertiveness that would alienate others. Where men are concerned, this is a serious impediment, but it can also be a problem between women and their children, and with other women.

Excessive effort to keep everybody happy at whatever cost to themselves prevents many women from deserved advancement in their work. It also causes many to fail to defend themselves when they should. For example, women often have put up with sexual harassment on the job because they didn't want to get the culprit in trouble. All relationships are not of equal depth, quality, or importance. Women need to be discriminating about which ones are actually worth preserving. They also need to realize the destructive consequences to others of tolerating behavior that should be stopped. The next woman who is harassed by the man you protected might be far more vulnerable than you, and serious psychological harm could ensue.

Women who have learned to be themselves can be sure

that when people like them it is a genuine response to a self they can maintain without trouble because it is real. The energy formerly diverted into *excessive* compliance has been freed for the far more rewarding task of cultivating those relationships which are really important.

The emphasis on the word "excessive" is important. As discussed in Chapters 3 and 4, men tend to pay too little attention to the personal factors in most situations. A very nice man, propelled to my office by his unhappy wife, said that he was perfectly happy in the marriage and couldn't understand what the fuss was about. I asked him, "Do you love her?" He replied, "Of course I do! She's marvelous!" I wondered how he could be happy since his beloved was not. My question, based on the obvious (to women) notion that unhappiness in either partner will be distressing to the other, came as a revelation to him.

While there may be some transitional discomfort, women need to realize that only claiming their true identity will enable them to become true partners with men in the conduct of human life. All relationships will thereby be enhanced.

SOME HELPFUL TECHNIQUES

Magical Wishes: If you could have three magical wishes, what would they be? Before reading further, ask yourself that question and make a note of your answers.

1st wish: . . . .
2nd wish: . . . .
3rd wish: . . . .

Women commonly give answers like, "I wish I had enough money in the bank to put my children through college"; "I wish my husband and I could afford a vacation in Scotland—he has always wanted to go there to look up his ancestors"; "I wish I had a grand piano so my

daughter would have a good instrument to practice on."
Such answers miss the point since they are actually
wishes for others, but many women claim that their
happiness is entirely contingent on that of their family.
No matter how much I explain, some women are unable
to imagine anything they might want *only* for themselves
without reference to any other relationship.

Others, in better shape with respect to their own identity, are able to give at least one or two wishes for
themselves. Then I ask what they have done about making them come true. Many are startled—even though
they know what they want, the idea of acting on the
knowledge has never occurred to them. Others say they
can't do it now—it must wait until the needs of everyone
else have been satisfied. Sometimes, as I hear the details,
this seems to be really true, but often it is just a ration-
alization.

These same women may be very assertive in their
home or workplace, sometimes to the point of being
domineering. Nevertheless, when their behavior is analyzed, very little of it is directed to their private goals. It
is to improve the lot of family members or fellow workers
or to advance the goals of an organization. When they do
work toward private goals, this is disguised as being for
someone else. We have all met bossy, interfering women
who are always doing things for someone else's good. If
they were able to admit that they deserved some private
space of their own, they might not have to encroach on
everyone else's to the same degree! Once women know
what they want *for themselves*, it is time enough to work
out whether or not it is possible to pursue that goal while
keeping other people's needs in mind.

Practice this "magical wish" exercise until you can
easily think of three things for yourself, and make at least
one of them come true without a twinge of guilt!

Imagination: Consider the first case I described in this

chapter. That woman had no model of shared responsibility to fall back on. The technique we used can be described as a planned daydream. She was to imagine a series of situations involving interaction with a man, in which a decision affecting them both was called for. Each situation was practiced several times, and she kept a written record of the imaginary action and conversations. The first time was her natural, unconsidered response to the scenario, such as I described in discussing her case. Then she was to imagine a different response, noting how she felt about changing her own role. She repeated the process until she was satisfied with the result. At first she had trouble imagining the man's role, being able only to see the stereotyped response she unthinkingly feared. This was handled by getting her to consider what she knew about his attitudes and to make a rational judgment about whether he was actually likely to behave as she expected. She soon realized that he was not. She could then develop her scenarios in accordance with the man's true personality, including being able to anticipate situations in which he might prefer some response she was not willing to make. She then practiced how to handle such situations. Gradually she was able to develop a model of shared responsibility she could fall back on instead of the "old tapes" that had governed her behavior at the start of our work together.

This technique can be adapted to fit nearly any situation. Writing down the scenarios is important. One can then go back and analyze the responses, checking them not only against the actual character of other people who may be involved but also against one's own goals. When problems are encountered, it is helpful to look for some of the hidden factors we have discussed in this chapter. This is especially important if none of the planned daydreams ever seems to come out "right."

Assertiveness Training: Workshops for assertiveness

training can be very helpful. Some women stay away because they confuse "assertiveness" with "aggressiveness" and fear someone is going to try to teach them to be nasty! This is not the point. Such workshops give opportunities for women to practice standing up for themselves appropriately, learning to express their true opinions without giving offense. Before signing up for such a workshop, it is probably a good idea to check it out with others who have already taken it, just to make sure that its goals will meet your special needs.

Counseling: If in spite of your best efforts with these techniques (or with others you may invent for yourself) you continue to have difficulty, some personal counseling may be in order. Many women shy away from that, fearing that to need counseling means something is seriously wrong with them. On the contrary. If you enjoyed swimming, wanted to do it better, but found that when you tried to dive all you could do was make a horrible splash, you would not feel badly about taking a few lessons from a swimming coach. This is really exactly the same.

REFERENCES

The material in this chapter is drawn from my psychiatric practice, with all case histories disguised to preserve confidentiality.

CHAPTER 6

What Will Be the Effect on the Family?

Many people believe that the changes suggested by "women's liberation" have a bad effect on the family. Their fears are aggravated by sensational stories of women who abandon husband and children in order to "find themselves." They worry about latchkey children, many from affluent families, who are alone because their mothers are out in the workplace "realizing their personal potential." They think a return to the old ways is essential to avoid the disintegration of family structure. Are they right? Or is the very institution of the family outmoded? Or, if it were properly implemented, could a new understanding of women's place in society strengthen the family?

THE FAMILY IS HERE TO STAY

First let us dispose of the idea that the family may be outmoded. Dr. Jerry Lewis has written a fine book, *How's Your Family?*, and the first sentence of the Introduction puts it well: "In a different and more perfect world, the family would be recognized as the unit of survival." Not only is it the unit of physical survival but of emotional survival as well. The social relationships prevailing in the family become the model for the child's notions of how the larger world is organized. As we saw in Chapter 1, enduring relationships in the home, where not only one's best but one's worst can be dealt with, are an essential ingredient in the formation of personal identity. It is true that psychosocial disturbances in the family can be damaging. In fact, all modern depth psychology is based on that insight, as illustrated by the cases cited in the last chapter.

That many families in our society are not doing a good job is obvious. But there is no evidence that abolishing the family would do anything but take us out of the frying pan into the fire. A general survey of human culture past and present shows that there are numerous styles of family organization, and many different kinds have been successful. Therefore, if we are dissatisfied with current models of family life, we have many options other than trying to turn the clock back or abolishing the family altogether.

THE HEALTHY FAMILY

Since the most basic layers of the adult personality are so heavily influenced by the family, to a degree that was not fully appreciated before the last fifty years or so, it is important to learn not only what are the damaging factors but also what features of family structure are beneficial. To that end Dr. Lewis and his colleagues have been studying healthy families for many years. Lewis says that "a healthy family is one that does two things well: *preserves the sanity and encourages the growth of the parents* and *produces healthy children*" (p. 4). Healthy children are those who have a high degree of individuality and autonomy. Immediately we can see the influence of culture. In some societies independence would not be considered the hallmark of the healthy child. But Lewis is writing about and for Americans. In this country young adults are not healthy if still "tied to mother's apron strings" or "under father's thumb," since such immature dependence makes it impossible for them to leave the original family, love someone else, and so start a new family of their own.

But much more interesting for our purposes is the kind of family that produces children who can meet this requirement. The relationship between the parents is the foundation. Many backgrounds are stressful, such as broken homes, poverty, or racial prejudice. No childhood is ideal. Therefore everyone comes to adulthood with certain vulnerabilities they necessarily bring into marriage. This is why the first clause of Lewis' definition emphasizes the importance of family structure in the emotional health and personal development of the married couple. He describes it this way:

> The stresses are inside the family and grow out of daily conflict, smoldering resentments, crushed hopes, and, in general, the failure of the family to provide the support, acceptance, and meaning that each individual needs. It is, then, within the family that the individual's mental health is finally determined. At the least, vulnerabilities are not converted to disabilities, but much more is possible. In some families the individual's vulnerabilities are undone, past hurts are healed, and the quest to fulfill one's potential is encouraged. (P. 5)

Two crucial elements in any marriage are power and intimacy. Power, in this sense, has to do with decision-making. Lewis discusses several patterns, including shared power and a dominant-submissive power system. What may come as a surprise is that *the healthiest families are those in which power is shared between husband and wife*. This has nothing to do with whether or not the mother works or stays home, with whether the father does or does not help with the housework, or with any of the other traditional sex-linked roles. The well-known 50-50 formula for successful marriage does not mean that all tasks are divided down the middle. It does mean that the views of both partners on any question are equally respected and that the competence of each is acknowledged. Either intuitively or by discussion, they will come to an understanding of who is better at what and trust each other's decisions in those areas of special competence. Neither rides roughshod over the other when disagreements arise.

Such an arrangement presupposes a high degree of trust between the partners, and this brings us to the question of intimacy. It is not easy to trust someone whom you do not know very well. Many spouses fall into a habit of communicating only superficially about the day-to-day problems of running a household. This is not enough. In healthy families husbands and wives share their deepest thoughts, their fears, joys, and daydreams. They know they will be listened to with sympathetic seriousness, will not be laughed at or rejected, nor will these personal revelations ever be thrown up to them later. Lewis calls this level of intimate communication "the mutual exchange of private worlds." One's spouse is one's closest friend.

The families in which one partner is always the boss are less successful, though some of these may work, at least for a time, if that pattern happens to meet the emotional needs of *both* partners. Sometimes this works for life. But it is less likely in such a system that the submissive partner will be able to be truly intimate, since it is hard to expose one's vulnerabilities to a permanent critic. Usually the dominant partner is unwilling to expose his (sometimes *her*) vulnerabilities either, for fear of undermining authority. It often happens that with increasing maturity the submissive partner (usually the woman) becomes less willing to remain in that role. If there are enough positive factors in the marriage, work with a counselor or with such programs as Marriage Encounter may accomplish the transition to a more mutual relationship. When such efforts fail, divorce or chronic unhappiness—even illness—is the unfortunate result. Needless to say, these outcomes are very hard on children, giving them models of the man/woman relationship which they may have trouble shaking when they themselves marry.

In the healthy family, children are carefully listened to. Their individuality is encouraged, but there is never any question that the parents are in charge. The expression of true feelings, including anger, is a natural part of the family pattern. Barring ordinary childhood rivalry, all are close and supportive of one another. The example of mutuality set by their parents gives children an excellent basis on which to form relationships, not only within the family but with others as well. When they are old enough to begin dating, they know that deep friendship is the key to successful relationships, and their chances of selecting the right partner for a happy marriage are greatly enhanced.

In order to take her part in the kind of intimate, responsible relationship that characterizes a healthy marriage, a woman must know who she is. The impediments to a consciousness of her own identity that have been discussed in previous chapters are also impediments to the sharing of either power or intimacy with a husband. It is true that some very successful marriages are contracted when the woman is so young that her identity is not yet fully established. If she has chosen the right mate, he will encourage her process of self-discovery, and all will be well. This must, naturally, be a mutual process. As we have seen, men have their own impediments to self-understanding, even if in many ways these are not so pervasive as they are for women. But a woman who is serious about her own growth will be supportive of a man struggling with his.

WOMAN'S WORK: AT HOME OR OUTSIDE?

The whole family suffers when energetic mothers who would rather be doing something else believe that the only appropriate objects of their attention are husband, home, and children. Such a woman may express her resentment by doing as little as possible and constantly complaining about how hard her lot is. This makes other family members feel angry, guilty, or both. Mutuality and intimacy are therefore impossible. Just as often, such a woman puts *too much* attention on her family. If she has to be stuck at home, by golly it's going to be the *perfect* home. She is critical and overcontrolling, never satisfied, intolerant of any mistakes by anyone, including herself. She may refuse to have baby-sitters or to go on vacations alone with her husband. She tolerates nothing but perfect manners, perfect grades, and perfect neatness in her children and can't understand when they drop out of school and go to live with messy friends who leave them alone. She drives her husband relentlessly and can't understand why he has a heart attack at forty; after all, she *insisted* that he eat properly and get regular exercise. She may complain that there is no mutuality or intimacy in the home but doesn't realize that she made both impossible.

A woman who knows who she is and what she wants out of life will handle the desire for outside work quite differently. In the first place, she will not feel guilty because she wants it. Managing a home is not easy and requires quite particular talents. Not all women are suited to it, any more than all men are suited to be engineers. A woman who knows herself will know what her talents are and will arrange her life so that she can exercise them appropriately. Very few people of either sex are so attached to their work that they willingly decide to forgo the joys and compromises of marriage in order to pursue it. And we no longer think it right for a man to assume his wife's willingness to submerge herself for his career. It has never occurred to anyone to expect a man to do that for his wife!

Contemporary men and women striving to establish healthy marriages will forget all about the old sex roles and devise *together* a pattern that suits them both. Sometimes this will mean permanent full-time household help, if the wife's work is sufficiently demanding. Sometimes the husband will voluntarily assume a large part of the household responsibilities. It is often forgotten that some men really enjoy managing a home, but they have never before had permission to do it. Many other patterns are possible, including some cases where husband and wife are in the same line of work and together fill *one* post, leaving each free to be home as needed.

Such practical solutions depend for their success on full cooperation between husband and wife, untinged by competitiveness at any level. If their relationship truly comes first, and has the qualities of intimacy and shared power that we have seen are essential, they will be able to manage harmoniously the serious compromises that may need to be made.

It is important to remember that the *quality* of time spent with children is far more important than the *quantity*. But this does not mean that they can be neglected much of the time (often by parking them in front of the television) and then be expected to participate happily when the parents eventually get around to them. They must be fully integrated into the family plans, where all take pride in each other's activities and all are equally important. Carefully chosen caretakers other than the parents can be a positive influence. It is good for children to realize from a young age that all adults are not alike, that different styles can be brought to many activities. If the mother does not feel secretly guilty about not being with her children 100 percent of the time, she is likely to have relatively little trouble getting and keeping competent household help. She will be unambiguously glad to have found someone to do essential work that she knows is not her strong suit and will be able to treat her helper with respect and gratitude. In most communities there are many people (still usually women) who would prefer to work in a home if only their employers didn't so often treat them like dirt!

But none of this means that women who truly prefer it should not stay home, either just for a few years, while the children are small, or permanently. Unfortunately, some feminist rhetoric has made women feel that to stay home is to be reduced to a menial level or sell out to the patriarchal system. That is nonsense. *True feminism gives women real choice. It does not impose a new set of restrictions in place of the old.*

And let's take another look at that word "menial." Much of the trouble our society is in today is because we do not realize that *all work is sacred.* Any work that cannot be viewed in that light is probably something that should not be done at all. Accomplishments are not what gives us value. In the sight of God there is no difference between the great artist, the waitress, the president of a corporation, the factory worker, the housewife, the scientist, the secretary, the college professor, or the person who cleans the bathrooms in the subway. The problem with considering some work to be menial, or beneath one's dignity, is that those who do that work come to be despised. And when others despise you, it is hard not to despise yourself eventually. This makes it difficult to do the work well, aggravating the vicious circle of looking down both on the work and the worker. Since they have done so much of the world's "lowly" work for so long, and therefore know best how necessary it is, women should refuse to participate in this destructive devaluation. And to apply such ideas to anything so essential to the entire human family as running a home is not only stupid but tragic.

The success of a woman's decision to work outside or at home depends on two things. First, she must know herself well enough to be sure about what she really wants to do, without feeling guilty about her choice. This takes considerable courage, especially if her decision runs counter to the customs of her community. Second, her decision must be accepted by her husband. By that I do *not* mean that she needs his permission. If the marriage is on the basis described above, she will be able to help him understand that her decision is *part of who she is*. The compromises, if any, will come as they plan *together* how to implement her decision while keeping the needs of the whole family in mind. In principle this is no different from the process required if the man's employer asks him to relocate to another city, or if the man himself wants a career change. In a healthy marriage he would never present such momentous ideas to his wife as settled facts. They would be possibilities to be jointly explored. The same thing is true for the wife.

Women who have abandoned husband and children to "find themselves," or who neglect home and children to "realize their personal potential," have failed at one or both of these tasks. Sometimes doubt or unresolved guilt about her choice is what makes her ride roughshod over her family in order to implement it. Sometimes she is a committed feminist and is insisting on outside work in order to "support the movement." These cases are really sad, since they covertly support the patriarchal values they are intended to repudiate, in which women do not get to choose for themselves but must do what some authority tells them. Sometimes she is still influenced by the problems discussed in Chapter 5 and so has no confidence that power and intimacy can be shared with a husband in such a way that rebellion and escape are unnecessary. She is probably a person who has never learned how to cooperate with anyone—she only knows how to boss or be bossed.

What about the husband's role in all this? Women who are not secure in their personal identity often fail to realize that, even when a husband is not naturally inclined to deal with family issues appropriately, his wife is in an excellent position to teach him how. She need not uncritically assume that the style of the family is up to him but can insist that a better way be found.

In summary, the real question is not *whether* a woman works in or out of the home but *how* she implements her choice. And it should not be forgotten that the decision to stay home after a family is accustomed to two incomes can be just as problematic as the decision to work away from home. Like any other family decision, this question will be resolved more smoothly when the marriage is on the healthy, mutual basis Lewis describes.

LONG-TERM EFFECTS ON CHILDREN

Under the old patriarchal system, women were not permitted to become fully mature self-determining adults. No matter how enlightened or benevolent a particular patriarch might be, there were limits beyond which the women under his care could not venture. For example, I know one family where all the women as far back as the late nineteenth century were college graduates, and many took advanced degrees. All were encouraged to work—until they got married. Then they were expected to subordinate themselves to their husbands' requirements, and it was assumed that this meant staying at home. Most of them were sufficiently well off to have household help, freeing them for some intellectual work. But this always took the form of assisting husbands in *their* work, never doing something on the women's own initiative. Until the current middle-aged generation, divorce was unthinkable, but several have now occurred.

What does that mean? It has something to do with the fact that the mothers of these women had all assumed that the husband was to be "head of the house" and the "obey" clause in their marriage ceremonies had been taken seriously. These women had all seen their mothers give in to bad decisions the fathers had made, sometimes confessing to their daughters that they *knew* the decision was wrong, but, after all, the important thing was to obey father and husband in order to preserve the integrity of the family. Changing conditions of modern society had given the younger women courage to decide that they would not let anything like that happen in their own lives. But when the time came, they did not know how to do anything but to submit or break up. One of them, in psychotherapy undertaken to deal with a failing marriage, went through a period of being extremely angry with her mother for not setting a better example. She said it would have been easier to forgive her had she been stupid or weak, but the opposite was the case, so the daughter could see no excuse for her behavior.

This family also illustrates the problems inherent in the attempt to maintain the fiction of male superiority. Several of these women have told me that one cause of their divorce was that they were more intelligent, and in one case better educated, than their husbands. Had their marriages been based on shared power and intimacy, this need not have been a problem. But because they felt obliged to play second fiddle all the time, they could not tolerate the pretense this so often required. Only one felt entitled to establish her own true identity, and she had no idea of how to go about it. All of them came to realize that the distorted views of the man/woman relationship which they had been taught had severely impaired their capacity to be realistic about mate selection.

The daughters of these women are now reaching marriageable age. They have no intention of repeating their mothers' and grandmothers' mistakes. One says she will never marry. Others have had a series of live-in arrangements in which they have painfully attempted to work through the problems before committing themselves to marriage. These decisions are also problematic, and one hopes that *their* daughters will not suffer any of the consequences.

The lesson to be drawn from this family history is that unless women claim their true identity they cannot embody an appropriate model of adult maturity for their children. I have described some of the effects on daughters, but the plight of sons is no better. A man who has been raised to believe that just because he is a man he is cock of the walk may have a hard time finding a young woman willing to play up to that. Even if he succeeds, the marriage is likely to be troubled one way or another. If he has avoided that antiquated belief, he still may develop a variety of problems if he has no model of true sharing with a woman to fall back on. Mothers who are confident, proud of their femininity, happy to be women, and neither jealous of nor in rebellion against their husbands' masculinity will do a much better job in helping both their boys and their girls to be comfortable and secure in their own sexual identity than will mothers who lack these qualities. The latter will unconsciously complicate their children's essential maturation.

6 8 4 33

A WORD ABOUT HUSBANDS

We live in transitional times. I have already said that the remains of patriarchy are in the air we breathe and that all women have to deal with it one way or another. The same is true for men. As I have indicated, their problems are simpler to the extent that they have no history of millennia of systematic socialization to take second place, even to the point of effacing their own identity if necessary. But they *do* have the serious problem of learning not to associate being in control with masculinity. This is extremely difficult. Women struggling to apply the lessons of this book in an already established marriage will do well to remember that and to be patient and understanding about their husbands' difficulties.

However, the next generation of husbands, now merely boys, also needs attention. It is extremely important to banish from the home many of the old distinctions on how boys and girls are treated. Both need to take their turn at *all* household chores. If your family has a custom of one member waiting on others at meals, boys must do this too. If the girls have to iron their own clothes, boys must be required to do the same. It may be desirable to have one child do a particular job all the time, but the decision should never be based on which jobs are "masculine" and which "feminine." Instead, it should be based on who does the job best or on who most needs to learn how to do it, regardless of sex.

The natural, sex-specific aggressiveness of boys should not be encouraged to take hostile forms. Guns and other implements of war are *not* suitable toys. Giving the other boy a black eye is *not* a sign of manliness. Running away is *not* always cowardly. Protecting the weak is one thing, and both boys and girls should be encouraged to do that within the limits of their capability. But being the aggressor under any circumstance is wrong. The term "sissy" must be abolished from everyone's vocabulary. If a boy is acting cowardly, his behavior must be properly named, but to use a word that implies the inferiority of the feminine is outrageous.

The way adult men and women treat each other is dependent on how they experience being a person of their own gender. And much more of that than is generally realized connects with their beliefs, unconscious as well as conscious, about sex. One of the valuable results of Freud's research was to teach us that, in however primitive a way, children form impressions about that from an extremely early age. Therefore, the right kind of sex education goes far beyond sitting children down at age ten or so and telling them the "facts of life." A crucial element is what they observe about the way their parents interact.

A whole book could be written about appropriate sex education. Whatever system is employed, it should aim at an attitude that sees sex neither as merely recreational nor as something nasty. Both those views are derived from an adolescent male perspective, unfortunately enshrined in things like the "Playboy Philosophy." The natural female response to sex begins with the overall relationship with the partner. This is something boys have to learn, since their own natural response begins at the physical level. Boys, in particular, need to understand that sex is something done *with*, not *to*, a partner. The use of the word "dirty" must be abolished. Even in homes where all think of themselves as having no unhealthy sexual inhibitions, most people refer to jokes about sex as "dirty." People who do this forget how literal and impressionable children are. We are all familiar with cases of girls who have been frightened either by their mothers or by some unfortunate experience into a fear of sex. It is less appreciated that the aggressive, exploitative, casual attitude of far too many men in our culture does just as much damage to boys' future ability to make good husbands because it is in essence immature. Unfortunately, some young women are now imitating that attitude. This results from a misunderstanding of true feminism, in which they see no alternative to being sexually exploited than to become themselves the exploiters. True mutuality has not been thought of, much less learned.

What a boy observes about how his mother functions in relation not only to his father but to other men (particularly important if she is a single parent) will have an incalculable effect on his adult ways of treating women. He will be a far better husband if he has seen his mother as a full person in her own right.

THE VERDICT

In terms of the future of the family, we have nothing to fear and much to gain from women's learning to claim and live out their full personal identity. The task of redressing the imbalance between the masculine and feminine principles, the importance of which was stressed in Chapter 4, is most effectively begun in the home. A wife whose competence is respected and whose feminine viewpoint is valued can influence the way a man functions in all his spheres of activity. A mother perceived by her children as a full, equal—though importantly different—partner to their father can go far in sparing them the problems discussed throughout this book.

REFERENCES

Lewis, Jerry M., M.D., *How's Your Family?* Brunner/Mazel, Inc., 1979. This highly recommended book is written for the general public and contains very helpful questionnaires to assist people in assessing the relationships in their own families. There is also an extremely helpful chapter on "What to Do" about problems you may identify.

CHAPTER 7

What Does Christianity Say About Women's Identity?

The seventeenth-century English poet John Milton described the proper relation between the sexes as "he for God, she for God in him." Many still think that expresses the Christian view. Others disagree strongly. Some feminists (both male and female) object to using masculine nouns and pronouns when referring to God, believing that a male God is at worst oppressive to women and even at best cannot speak to their spiritual needs. Attempts to revive interest in the Virgin Mary are usually viewed as a last-ditch attempt by ecclesiastical patriarchs to enforce a model of feminine submissiveness. Paul is quoted and misquoted by all parties to these debates. Is there a middle ground? Does the claim that men and women should relate as cooperative equals have any theological support?

CREATION IN THE IMAGE OF GOD

Genesis states that humanity was created in the image of God. What does this "image of God" include? Doesn't it only refer to some aspect of the soul that has nothing to do with sex? The passage reads: "let us make man in our image, in the likeness of ourselves . . . male and female

he created them." First we note that God refers to himself
in the plural. The infinite richness and diversity of God's
nature is expressed by the many names for him used in
the Old Testament. Significantly, the particular God-
name used in this passage is Elohim, which in Hebrew is
a feminine noun with a masculine plural ending. Although there is no denying the masculine, patriarchal
aspect of God throughout the Old Testament, the feminine aspect is also present, though largely overlooked in
post-Reformation theology. The Hebrew word for the
"spirit of God" which moved "over the face of the wa-
ters" at creation is *ruach*, a feminine noun. God's out-
reach toward his people is nearly always described in
feminine terms. For instance, in the many passages where
God is said to "stretch out his hand" to his people, the
feminine word *yad* (hand) is used.

From this evidence we may conclude that when God
made humanity in his own image, he was expressing
something about his own nature. On his plane of being it
is a unity, but in order to make it manifest in creation he
differentiated it into the forms we know as male and
female. So one way of answering the question "Who are
we?" is to say that each woman and each man is a unique
reflection of the image of God and that sexuality is an
integral *part* of that image.

Because of sin, both personal and corporate, and because of immaturity, again both personal and corporate,
that divine image in each of us is at least tarnished, if not
actually covered with heaps of sinful human refuse. The
ways in which men and women mistreat each other are
part of that sin. In God's nature, the many different
elements (including, but of course not limited to, what
we experience as sexuality) cooperate so harmoniously
that God is truly described as One. God's original intention must have been for men and women to cooperate
similarly, or he would never have decreed that "they two

shall become one." The other creation account in Genesis says that woman was created from one of Adam's ribs. Some people see in this an implication of female inferiority. But since the story specifically states that Eve was created to be *like* Adam, and to be a *partner* to him, that interpretation, whether made by chauvinist patriarchs or by angry feminists, is obviously in error.

In trying to find the answer to the question "Who am I, really?" the untarnished reflection of God's image is what each of us should be looking for, men and women alike. And we may be sure that to the extent we find it, our sinful tendency to contribute to the "battle of the sexes" will be eliminated. The divine model, whether we consider the Old Testament God-names or the Christian Trinity, is not one of domination or competition but of creative harmony.

PATRIARCHY: GOD-GIVEN OR MAN-MADE?

Patriarchy is an almost universal social form that arose independently all over the world about seven or eight thousand years ago. It was well established long before the time when even the oldest part of the Old Testament was written. Customs everyone takes for granted are not questioned, and a reading of the biblical narrative shows that patriarchy is in this category. Many other customs were questioned. Through the prophets, God continually urged his people to change, to be renewed, to overthrow that which had degenerated or was simply outworn. God's plan is dynamic, not static. He constantly calls us to greater maturity.

Full personal maturity requires a sophisticated conscience. Upholding the received standards of family, tribe, nation—or even church—is not enough. The life and teachings of Jesus require from us a higher standard than the old law. He taught that each person should be individually responsible directly to God. This was misunderstood by the religious authorities of the time. They feared that so much freedom would lead to chaos. Jesus tried to explain by saying that he had come not to abolish the law but to fulfill it. He wanted people to look at the *principles* behind the rules. Sometimes in order to be true to a principle, it is necessary to break a rule. His attitude toward such things as healing on the Sabbath illustrates this.

Jesus taught that the Kingdom of God is not defined by the social or legal conditions of the heavenly community but by the spiritual maturity of its individual members. How else can we understand the saying that the Kingdom is within? No longer could people excuse immoral behavior by saying "I was only following orders." They were expected to have thought the matter out for themselves. But how? The instructions he gave were simple, if not easy. He quoted the summary of the law, already given in the Old Testament: "Love the Lord your God with all your heart, soul, mind, and strength" and "love your neighbor as yourself" (Mark 12:30, 31, JB; adapted).

Alicia Craig Faxon has written a fine book, *Women and Jesus*, in which she demonstrates that Jesus did not follow the patriarchal rules of his time. For instance, in those days men did not converse with women outside their family. Jesus did. He took for granted that women were to be included as independent participants in the Kingdom, and this made him a radical feminist in his time (and ours!).

His transcendent vision of fully responsible individuals, men and women alike, was shared by Paul, as we shall see below. There is a good deal of evidence to show that in the earliest years of Christianity women enjoyed an equality with men that they are only now beginning to reappropriate. But we must remember that at that time Christians were a weird minority, frequently persecuted by the dominant culture, on which their impact was gradual. When Emperor Constantine was converted in the fourth century, he had his entire army baptized, and Christianity then became the state religion. This stopped the persecutions, but the uninstructed new "converts" did not change their ways. So it is not surprising that patriarchy continued to be the prevailing pattern within which Christian traditions were developed.

Originally, patriarchy was a complex hierarchical system in which every person had an assigned place, and God was thought to communicate directly only with kings, priests, and prophets. Personal liberty for *anyone* was slow to develop. In spite of the New Testament insistence that human distinctions of status between male and female, or free citizens and slaves, were not part of the divine order, it took eighteen centuries for Christians to realize that slavery was *wrong*. During the arguments about the abolition of slavery in the last century, many sincere Christians quoted the Bible in support of their view that slavery was ordained by God and that only the way slaves were treated could be a matter for discussion. No responsible person would dream of such an interpretation of Scripture today.

In a society where one group is defined even partially as hierarchically superior to another, the qualities and values of the secondary group cannot be fully developed on their own terms. This stunts the personal growth of the members and also deprives the dominant group of the advantages that would accrue from having mature partners. As Abraham Lincoln put it, the master/slave relationship demeans not only the slave but the master. The religious issue is that the dominant group does not perceive the subordinate group as neighbors whom they must love as they love themselves. At least in principle, we now understand this point clearly in terms of slavery, even though it is taking a long time for the descendants of slaveowners to treat the descendants of slaves according to the full meaning of our Lord's instructions. But we can see from this example that the principles would apply to *any* subordinate group, including women. Our developing understanding of the Christian faith, therefore, not only does not support the continuation of male dominance but actually requires that we work together to eliminate it.

WHAT ABOUT PAUL AND THE EARLY CHURCH?

Many have noticed the apparent inconsistencies in Paul's statements about the role of women in family, society, and church. Unfortunately, interpreters have tended to quote, usually out of context, those passages which support their own beliefs, conveniently ignoring the rest. There are several things wrong with this approach. The Bible was given to us as a *foundation* for thought, not as a *substitute* for it. It is not enough just to follow a set of rules covering all facets of human behavior, even supposing that such a coherent set could actually be found there. Jesus spent much time arguing against precisely that attitude. It helps to realize that Paul was considered difficult from the start, and a comment about that is included in Scripture itself. II Peter 3:16 says about Paul's letters, "There are some things in them hard to understand, which the ignorant and unstable twist to their own destruction." If those who knew him had trouble, we should certainly not expect any simple interpretation now to be satisfactory.

To understand Paul we must pay attention to the social conditions of the time when the letters were written. We also need to remember that he was not writing general essays but letters to specific congregations with particular problems. Unfortunately, we do not have the other half of the correspondence. It has taken considerable scholarly research to piece together a reasonable picture of precisely what Paul was talking about.

Fortunately, a book called *The Moral Teachings of Paul* has recently been written for the general public by just such a scholar, Victor Furnish. He begins by warning us not to treat Paul either as a "sacred cow" or as a "white elephant"! He puts most emphasis on Romans, I and II Corinthians, Galatians, Philippians, I Thessalonians, and Philemon, since nearly all scholars in the field agree that Paul himself wrote those letters. Ephesians, Colossians, I and II Timothy, and Titus were probably written by early followers. Furnish gives a lively picture of the culture of the time, including the beliefs then prevalent in pagan society.

The conclusions Furnish draws about what Paul *really* says are entirely consistent with what has been put forward in this book. They are based not only on a careful examination of the texts but also on an analysis of Paul's encounters with the women mentioned in the letters. Paul lays "consistent emphasis on the mutuality of the marriage relationship. Paul regards the husband and wife as equal partners." Also, Paul has a deep concern for the *quality* of the relationship. "Each partner must affirm and support the existence and the personhood of the other." Equally striking is Paul's flexibility in handling individual situations. Paul emphasizes that the good order of the Christian community and undivided devotion to God is paramount, and that individuals do not all reach that goal in the same way.

For some, including Paul himself, the single life is preferable. That point deserves special emphasis, since it has so often been said that marriage and motherhood are the only suitable vehicles for the Christian woman's life. Contrary to what most Protestants think, Roman Catholic women always had some advantage here, since entering a convent provided an alternative. In many cases, in spite of the often harsh restrictions of monastic life, this allowed far more scope for personal development than marriage, especially if the husband was an autocratic patriarch. But convents had not been invented in Paul's day, and he unequivocally supports the independent single life for women as well as for men.

HOW CAN A MALE GOD SPEAK TO WOMEN'S NEEDS?

Christians insist that God is *personal*. This is true, but sometimes we take it too literally and begin to imagine that God is a *person*. We forget that the Bible also has *impersonal* images, such as the burning bush, the fiery serpent, and the rock. God's nature is infinitely mysterious, but in order to communicate with us he has made himself known in personal terms. Often he is our parent, and that New Testament image is one *we* have singled out for special emphasis. But there are other personal images we have fallen into the bad habit of neglecting.

One such image running through both the Old and New Testaments is *sexual*. Israel is described as the spouse of God, the church as the bride of Christ. The sexually explicit Song of Songs is included in the Bible. We have consistently failed to understand the significance of this image, because during the Christian era we came to think of the body as inferior and its natural passions as shameful, if not dangerous. The ancient Hebrews did not have this problem. For them, a human being was an indivisible psychophysical unity, of which sexuality was a clear part, given by God at creation. Like any other human activity, it was of course subject to the distortions of sinful misuse, but it was not *inherently* inferior. There is nothing, anywhere in the Bible, to support the frequent view that grew up gradually during the Christian era, that the sexual instinct is somehow sinful. How Christians developed that idea is an interesting chapter in church history, too complex to discuss here. But the point is that *it is not scriptural*!

We saw that God has, as part of his *personal* aspect, feminine qualities as well as masculine. In Chapter 3 we saw that one task of human growth is to integrate the feminine and masculine components of the psyche. Jesus did that perfectly. Careful reading of the Gospels reveals that he fit no sexual stereotypes of any era. Therefore our human psychological androgyny is part of being created in God's image. And part of what it means to recover the purity of that image, now contaminated by sin, is to learn to appreciate, value, and develop *both* qualities, using each where appropriate according to our Lord's example.

Before the Reformation, the feminine aspect of God was more generally appreciated. Lady Julian of Norwich, a fourteenth-century English mystic, wrote that "the human mother will suckle her child with her own milk, but our beloved mother, Jesus, feeds us with himself." In the eleventh century, Anselm of Canterbury also referred to Jesus our Mother, seeing him as giving birth to Christian souls through his passion and death. Both male and female mystics frequently described their deepest experiences of prayer in explicitly sexual images, perceiving themselves as the feminine partner in the intercourse with God. To modern Protestants, such passages seem peculiar if not actually perverse. But that says more about our view of sex than it does about the appropriateness of such experiences of God.

With that in mind, how should we interpret the sexual metaphors describing God's relationship to us? First we must clear our minds of the degraded and oversimplified concept of sexuality that pervades our culture. It is *not* just a recreational end in itself, as secular society would now have us believe, any more than it is something nasty. Both ideas are wrong, both lead to a misunderstanding of

sex, and both contribute to difficulties in human relationships. We have mistakenly projected our human distortions of sexuality onto the scriptural metaphors. That is
why we decided they must not be intended literally but
only in some "spiritual" sense. But what happens when
we look at them anew?

The principle of wholeness, of at-one-ment, of union, is
vividly conveyed by images of sexuality. These biblical
images cannot be reduced to the merely physical aspect
of sex. The intermingling of masculine and feminine is
present at all levels. The church, as the bride of Christ,
includes both men and women. Both, therefore, are to
take a "feminine" posture toward God. This is an attitude
of receptive trust. It has nothing to do with the devalued
caricatures of passivity often currently associated with
the feminine. But just as men are physically more powerful than women, and therefore potentially frightening,
so God is more powerful than any person, hence the "fear
of the Lord." How, then, can a true relationship be
established? Love is the answer. When we are convinced
we are loved, we can trust. That is how women overcome
the fear of the physically powerful male; it is also how
human persons of either sex overcome their fear of the
powerful God: "We love him because he first loved us."
The parallel is precise. But there is more.

We are co-creators with God. Because he endowed us
with free will, he cannot bring about the glorious end
point of his Kingdom without our cooperation. The initiatory power that calls matter into being belongs to God.
This is precisely parallel to the man's role in reproduc-
tion—without it no fertilization can take place. But the
woman's role is just as essential, since she must receive
and nourish the seed. Similarly, humanity must receive
God's holy inspirations so that we can play our necessary
part in bringing in the Kingdom. This is why I find it
appropriate to refer to God as "he."

The scriptural images show God's attempt to establish a loving and fruitful relationship with humanity. Perhaps the most striking example is his divine impregnation of the Virgin Mary. To be sure, God is sometimes described as angry when we reject his efforts. But over and over, he tries again to win us through love, to secure our willing cooperation in the task of establishing the Kingdom. He really *wants* to establish the co-creator relationship with us. The story of Hosea and his faithless wife makes this point beautifully.

Our trouble is that the descriptions by male theologians, especially since the Reformation, have presented God as rapist, not loving spouse and co-creator. No wonder many women are angry! They see the terrible imbalance between masculine and feminine that was discussed in human terms earlier in this book. When they hear God spoken of as "he," what comes to mind is not *ideal* masculinity but a masculinity distorted by human sin. Still, to deny God's masculinity aggravates the imbalance. The human posture toward God must be receptive so that our energy, enlivened by his, can work toward the creation of the good world. We can't do that right if we minimize God's initiatory activity. If we render him impotent, nothing will get created, and an angry humanity will respond just the way women do in that situation. Far more fruitful would be a thorough study of God's perfect model. Women should then hold that up to men as the standard by which they must try to live.

A NEW LOOK AT THE VIRGIN MARY

Ever since she reputedly appeared to an illiterate Mexican peasant in 1531, the Virgin Mary has been the special saint of the Mexican poor. This devotion, which spread to the rest of the continent, is a powerful factor in the Latin-American revolutionary fervor to right the wrongs of the

oppressed. Our political leaders obviously do not understand this element of the chronic unrest south of our
border. The sociologist Nora Kinzer says that North
American interpreters are "most often Protestant North
American males who see Latin America through a Cal-
vinist glass darkened by male supremacy." Some aspect
of the feminine principle (described in Chapter 3) is
always involved in any liberation movement, both as
inspiration and as that which must be liberated. This
provokes severe patriarchal backlash when traditional
power structures are threatened, and that is a tragically
neglected feature of the South American political situation.

Jesus said, "Happy are you when men shall revile and
persecute you for my sake." Ignorant secular critics have
seen this as evidence for the view that Christianity pro-
motes a slave mentality. Others call it neurotic, sometimes equating that with "feminine" since women are
claimed to be "naturally masochistic." These views completely miss the point. People are most likely to be
persecuted when they resist the power of dominant op-
pressors and stand up for their personal rights and beliefs. Jesus was encouraging his followers to do just that.
Love is the only appropriate principle of relatedness.
When power is substituted for it, as in our decadent
patriarchy, the most basic tenets of religion are being
violated. The only power appropriate in this world is the
power of God, which can flow through us when we live
the exemplary life of Love. The life of Martin Luther
King makes these points absolutely clear. Though persecuted to death, he *was* happy and blessed.

Interest in the cult of the Virgin Mary is now rising just
because we so desperately need the feminine to be a
balancing force strong enough to enable the masculine to
find expression that is not destructive. This cult has taken
many forms over the centuries, ranging from seeing Mary

as almost divine to seeing her as an unimportant figure *except* (what male arrogance lies in that word "except"!) as the mother of Jesus. But now there is a growing view of her as a real woman, "answering Yes to life, Yes to humanity, Yes to God's invitation. A new Mary is emerging . . . who is the personification and prototype of the Christian mission—a woman who humanizes the world by being present where needed."

This has promise. But for that promise to be fulfilled, both Protestants and Roman Catholics must give up their heretical ideas of Mary. The Protestant heresy is to despise or ignore her. This attitude is both cause and result of the Protestant hypermasculinization of God. The Roman heresy desexualizes her by insisting that she remained virgin all her life. In view of the clear biblical references to Jesus' siblings, and the constant reference to Joseph as her husband, this claim is highly unlikely. It did not arise until the third century and is not part of the earliest tradition. Mary and Joseph were good Jews in a Jewish culture, and given the Jewish views of sex and marriage it simply does not make sense to say that she remained virgin all her life.

If Mary is a real woman, how can she be asexual? I believe that idea expresses the patriarchal need to devalue sex in order to maintain the notion of female inferiority. When sex is fully accepted as an integral part of the way God created us all, then one's sexual partner must be recognized as an equal. The desexualization of Mary disempowers her symbolic value as one who says yes either to life or to humanity, and makes her yes to God mere submission to the superpatriarch. This leaves men free for phallic domination of women and nature, with contempt for them because they permit it. Because they were lifelong virgins, the Holy Perfect woman and celibate female saints are spared the full measure of this contempt. The astonishing male faculty of compartmentalization allows men to revere Mary as a nice holy lady who has nothing to do with the "real male world." Others dismiss her cult as a sentimental necessity for female worshipers, and perhaps a good submissive role model for them too. But this is not her message!

The real Mary is a real woman in every particular. This means taking her sexuality seriously, including her life with Joseph, on the same plane as her impregnating encounter with the Holy Spirit. The Mary who can be an inspiration to women in our difficult transitional time is the perfect model of a woman who says yes to life and *who is not afraid to be unconventional in the service of her true destiny.*

CONCLUSION

Although this book has focused on the identity of women, I hope it is clear by now that modification of men's identity is also implied. Since *both* men and women are created in the image of God, and since each partakes to some extent of the nature of the other, changes women make cannot help changing men as well. If women learn to think of themselves as the neglected half of the image of God, they will never again accept assignment to second place in the home or in society. Men need relief from the sinful burden of imagining that they carry a superior version of the divine image. That self-important fantasy is endangering the whole human family. So both men and women need to do serious work on this question of identity.

All spiritual masters, and even some modern psychologists, tell us that we cannot find our truest identity apart from God. In a wonderful little book, *The Undiscovered Self,* the great Swiss psychiatrist Carl Jung argues most persuasively that without religion people are bound to sink into mass-mindedness, to become in some important degree mere unreflecting members of a herd. This is because, without a standard beyond the human plane, it is not possible to resist group pressure for long. And human group pressure, as we have seen, tends to bring everyone down to the lowest common, sinful denominator. Furthermore, the larger the group, the lower the level. But persons who earnestly try to measure their conduct in terms of the divine standard will have the courage to be in the minority when necessary. They will also have the humility to know that being in the majority is no guarantee of being in the right.

There is no danger that so much mature individuality might disrupt the human community. When rooted in God, individuality can never deteriorate into "do your own thing, let's have no hassles," let the chips fall where they may. Instead, the result will be full participation in the human community through loving and redeeming action in the world. The great spiritual masters have all said that is the final test of development: Truly knowing oneself, and finding one's truest self in God, makes true love of neighbor not only possible but inevitable.

Only the eternally new message of the gospel can heal our distorted views of God (as all-male, all-female, or sexless), of ourselves (as either superior or inferior by reason of gender), and the world of the opposite sex (as either superior or inferior). If we accept that healing, then we can stop the sin of trying to have power over one another. We can then get on with the life of fruitful equality, in which no one is either master or slave but all are neighbors sustained by the love of God.

REFERENCES

Faxon, Alicia Craig, *Women and Jesus*. United Church Press, 1973.

Furnish, Victor Paul, *The Moral Teaching of Paul*. Abingdon Press, 1979. This wonderful little book is written for the general reader. I have used only the parts relating to women, but the rest of Paul's teachings are also covered. It has excellent references and suggestions for further reading. Its format is well adapted for either individual or group study.

Jung, Carl Gustav, *The Undiscovered Self*. Little, Brown & Co., 1958. Also available in paperback and in the Collected Works of C. G. Jung. He was writing about the dangerous political situation prior to World War II, but everything in this little book applies with still more force today.

Kinzer, Nora Scott, "Sexist Sociology," *The Center Magazine*, May/June 1974. Prof. Kinzer gives an interesting contrast between the position of women in North and South America, not, surprisingly, entirely to our advantage.

The following two books are also recommended for those interested in a broad theological perspective on human identity.

Macquarrie, John, *In Search of Humanity*. Seabury Press, 1983. This book, though written by a professor of theology at Oxford University, is not too technical for the general reader. It is thoroughly based not only in the scholarly competence of the author but in a warm appreciation for the particulars of contemporary life.

Micks, Marianne H., *Our Search for Identity*. Fortress Press, 1982. This excellent book by a professor at Virginia Theological Seminary has a lot to say not only about identity in general but also about men and women. With the minor exception of the comments on Jung, it is both illuminating and practical.